SYDNEY GRAY

The Confident Candidate

Tips to Stand Out from the Competition, and Strategies for Leaving a Lasting Impression

Copyright © 2024 by Sydney Gray

All rights reserved. No part of this publication may be reproduced, stored or transmitted in any form or by any means, electronic, mechanical, photocopying, recording, scanning, or otherwise without written permission from the publisher. It is illegal to copy this book, post it to a website, or distribute it by any other means without permission.

First edition

This book was professionally typeset on Reedsy. Find out more at reedsy.com

Contents

Introduction	1
Chapter 1: Understanding the Modern Job Market	7
Chapter 2: Crafting a Stand-Out Resume	14
Chapter 3: Perfecting the Cover Letter	21
Chapter 4: Researching the Company and Industry	28
Chapter 5: Preparing for Common Interview Questions	37
Chapter 6: Mastering the Art of Non-Verbal Communication	43
Chapter 7: Answering Tough Interview Questions	49
Chapter 8: Standing Out in Virtual Interviews	56
Chapter 9: Asking Insightful Questions	63
Chapter 10: Demonstrating Soft Skills	68
Chapter 11: Following Up After the Interview	74
Chapter 12: Interviewing for Leadership Roles	80
Chapter 13: Handling Group and Panel Interviews	88
Chapter 14: Overcoming Nerves and Anxiety	96
Chapter 15: Leveraging Your Network for Success	103
Chapter 16: Preparing for Behavioral Assessments	112
Conclusion: Your Road to Success	120

Introduction

Why Standing Out Matters

In today's hyper-competitive job market, it is no longer enough to simply meet the qualifications for a role. The sheer volume of candidates applying for any given position means that even the most talented individuals can be overlooked if they fail to differentiate themselves. Companies now use a variety of tools—from automated applicant tracking systems (ATS) to intricate behavioral assessments—to filter out candidates who do not immediately shine. This reality creates an environment where blending in can be detrimental to your career progression.

To understand why standing out matters, it's essential to grasp the broader dynamics of modern hiring. Over the last decade, the job market has transformed. The rise of online job boards, professional networks like LinkedIn, and recruiting technologies has dramatically increased the number of applicants for any given role. A hiring manager today might receive hundreds, even thousands, of resumes for a single job posting. In this environment, recruiters spend just seconds skimming each resume before deciding whether to move the candidate forward in the process. This is why differentiation is key. If you don't quickly stand out, you risk being relegated to the "no" pile without ever having the opportunity to showcase your full potential.

The Noise of the Modern Job Market

The digital age has made applying for jobs easier, but it has also made it more impersonal. With the rise of one-click applications, candidates can submit their resumes to dozens of jobs in minutes, but this also means that hiring managers are flooded with applications, many of which are not even relevant to the position. This avalanche of resumes leads to a dehumanized process where resumes are filtered based on keywords and quick scans. For job seekers, this means the margin for error is razor-thin, and the importance of standing out becomes even more critical.

Furthermore, many companies now rely on ATS to scan and rank resumes before a human ever sees them. If your resume doesn't include the right keywords, you may not even make it past this automated gatekeeper. ATS systems prioritize resumes that closely match the job description, which means that generic resumes are less likely to be noticed. The cold, algorithm-driven process can be disheartening, but it also underscores the need to be intentional about how you present yourself from the very start.

The Importance of Personal Branding

In a saturated market, personal branding is one of the most effective tools for standing out. Your personal brand is how you present yourself both online and offline—essentially, it's your professional reputation. It encompasses everything from your resume and LinkedIn profile to how you communicate in interviews and follow-up emails. In an age where recruiters often check candidates' social media profiles, personal branding extends beyond what you say about yourself; it's about the narrative you create and how others perceive you.

Consider this: if a hiring manager is deciding between two equally qualified candidates, the one with a clear personal brand—someone who demonstrates passion, vision, and alignment with the company's values—will have the edge. Standing out is not about gimmicks or being flashy; it's about presenting a consistent, authentic narrative that makes you memorable.

Many job seekers neglect this step, focusing solely on checking off the boxes of required qualifications. While having the right technical skills and experience is vital, employers are increasingly looking for candidates who bring more than just competence to the table. They want to see energy, enthusiasm, and a forward-thinking attitude that will positively impact their team. By developing a strong personal brand, you are already separating yourself from those who rely solely on their qualifications to do the talking.

Cultural Fit and Differentiation

One of the main reasons differentiation matters so much today is that companies are putting more emphasis on cultural fit. Employers are not just looking for someone who can do the job; they want someone who will thrive within their organization's culture. In fact, cultural fit is often considered just as important as technical skills, if not more so.

This shift in priorities gives candidates the perfect opportunity to differentiate themselves, as it is much harder to evaluate cultural fit based on a resume alone. Employers are looking for people who align with their values and who will bring something unique to their team dynamic. To stand out, you need to demonstrate that you not only have the technical skills to succeed but also the emotional intelligence, adaptability, and vision that will benefit the organization in a broader sense.

Standing out also involves showing how your unique perspective, experiences, and background can add value to the company. Whether it's your understanding of the latest trends in the industry, a particularly creative problem-solving approach, or an ability to work across different departments, highlighting how you differ from other candidates is crucial. This not only positions you as a strong candidate but also makes it easier for hiring managers to remember you when making their final decision.

How This Book Will Help You

The purpose of this book is to provide you with actionable strategies that will help you stand out at every stage of the job search process. Whether you are a recent graduate looking for your first job, a seasoned professional aiming for a career change, or someone climbing the corporate ladder, this book will guide you through the steps needed to differentiate yourself in a meaningful and memorable way.

In the following chapters, we'll break down each component of the job application process, offering tips and insights that go beyond the basics. From crafting a compelling resume and cover letter to mastering the art of the interview, this book is designed to equip you with the tools and mindset needed to outshine the competition. We'll focus on practical advice, with real-world examples that show you how to apply these techniques in a way that feels authentic and sustainable.

Crafting a Standout Resume and Cover Letter

Your resume and cover letter are the first impression you'll make, and they are often the deciding factor in whether you get invited to an interview. Unfortunately, many job seekers treat these documents as formalities, when they should be viewed as critical marketing tools. In this book, you'll learn how to craft a resume that not only passes ATS filters but also tells your professional story in a way that resonates with hiring managers. We'll also dive deep into writing cover letters that stand out—cover letters that go beyond repeating your resume and show why you are uniquely qualified for the job.

We'll teach you how to tailor your resume and cover letter to each position, emphasizing the importance of customization. In a sea of generic applications, the personalized, thoughtful approach will immediately set you apart. You'll also learn the art of highlighting achievements in a way that demonstrates the value you've brought to previous roles and how that experience can benefit your potential employer.

INTRODUCTION

Preparing for Interviews

Once you've made it to the interview stage, the stakes get higher. Now, it's no longer about your qualifications on paper but about how well you can communicate your value in person. Many candidates lose opportunities at this stage because they fail to prepare thoroughly or get overwhelmed by nerves. This book will guide you through the interview process, helping you master everything from body language to answering tricky questions with confidence and poise.

We'll also cover how to prepare for different types of interviews, including panel and virtual interviews, both of which have become increasingly common in today's job market. You'll learn how to navigate these formats while ensuring that your personality and expertise shine through.

Post-Interview Strategies

The interview isn't the end of the road—it's just another step in the process. Many candidates neglect post-interview follow-up, missing an opportunity to stand out further. This book will teach you how to follow up in a way that keeps you top-of-mind for the hiring manager without coming off as pushy. You'll learn how to write a thoughtful thank-you note that reinforces your interest and qualifications, as well as when and how to check in after the interview to demonstrate continued enthusiasm for the role.

In addition to follow-up strategies, we'll also explore how to handle rejection. Rejections, while discouraging, can offer invaluable feedback and provide a chance to build relationships for future opportunities. By leveraging rejections as learning experiences and networking moments, you can turn a "no" today into a potential "yes" tomorrow.

Emphasizing Soft Skills

While technical skills may get you the interview, soft skills—such as communication, emotional intelligence, and teamwork—are what will ultimately set you apart. Employers increasingly value candidates who can demonstrate emotional intelligence and adapt to different work environments. This book will show you how to emphasize your soft skills in a way that complements your technical abilities, making you a well-rounded candidate.

Positioning Yourself for Leadership Roles

Finally, for those looking to move into leadership roles, standing out requires a different strategy. This book will teach you how to position yourself as a leader, even if you're not currently in a managerial role. You'll learn how to demonstrate strategic thinking, decision-making, and a vision that aligns with the company's long-term goals. Leadership isn't just about having a title; it's about exhibiting the traits and behaviors that inspire others to follow you.

Your Competitive Edge

In conclusion, this book is about empowering you to stand out in a crowded field. The job market is competitive, but by taking a strategic approach and differentiating yourself, you can move beyond being just another applicant. Throughout this book, you will find the tools, tactics, and mindset shifts needed to turn your job search into a career-defining opportunity. By embracing these strategies, you will not only increase your chances of landing the job but also position yourself for long-term career success.

Chapter 1: Understanding the Modern Job Market

The Shift in Hiring Practices

The hiring landscape has undergone a significant transformation in recent years, driven largely by advances in technology, globalization, and changes in workplace culture. Gone are the days when a job application consisted solely of mailing in a paper resume or physically dropping it off at the company's office. Today, recruitment is a digital-first process, with AI, automation, and online platforms playing an increasingly critical role in how companies source, screen, and hire candidates. For job seekers, this shift has created both opportunities and challenges, as it demands a new approach to standing out in a sea of applications.

The shift in hiring practices has been largely propelled by the rise of Applicant Tracking Systems (ATS), which allow companies to streamline the hiring process by automating the initial stages of recruitment. ATS software is designed to scan and rank resumes based on specific keywords and criteria. It filters out applicants who do not meet the predetermined standards set by the employer, making it easier for hiring managers to focus on the most qualified candidates. This technology has been a game changer for companies, especially those receiving thousands of applications for a single position. However, it also means that job seekers must now consider not only the human audience but also the algorithms when crafting their resumes.

The Role of AI and Automation in Recruitment

AI and automation have changed the way recruiters approach hiring, moving it from a manual, time-consuming process to one that is data-driven and highly efficient. Recruitment tools powered by artificial intelligence can do everything from sourcing candidates to conducting preliminary interviews through chatbots and automated questionnaires. This has allowed companies to cast a wider net and make data-backed hiring decisions, often in a fraction of the time it once took.

One major way AI is used in recruitment is through resume screening. Instead of manually reading through hundreds of resumes, recruiters rely on AI tools to sift through the data, highlighting those that match the job description based on keywords, experience, and even specific skills. For job seekers, this underscores the importance of customizing each resume to the job listing. Using generic or broad language can result in your resume being passed over because it lacks the specific keywords that the AI is programmed to identify.

Beyond screening resumes, AI is also used to analyze data from job postings, company websites, and even social media to predict which candidates will be the best fit. Machine learning algorithms can assess a candidate's past performance, personality traits, and cultural fit based on the digital footprint they leave behind. Tools like predictive analytics help recruiters make more informed decisions, but they also demand that job seekers be aware of their online presence and how it might impact their chances.

Moreover, AI-driven tools have made virtual interviewing more common. Chatbots, for instance, are now being used for preliminary interviews, where they ask candidates standard questions to gauge their qualifications and fit for the role. While these interactions are relatively simple, they allow companies to quickly weed out unqualified applicants before moving on to more personalized interviews with human recruiters.

For job seekers, this automation poses both a challenge and an opportunity. On the one hand, it means that every interaction—whether submitting a resume, answering an automated interview question, or even posting on social media—needs to be optimized for the digital eyes of AI algorithms. On the other hand, it levels the playing field, giving candidates who might not have had the right connections a better chance to get noticed based on their skills and experience.

The Impact of Online Platforms on Job Searching

Online platforms like LinkedIn, Indeed, and Glassdoor have become the primary tools for job seekers and employers alike. These platforms serve as one-stop shops for job postings, company reviews, and networking opportunities. Their ubiquity means that job seekers must now navigate these platforms strategically to stand out and make meaningful connections.

LinkedIn, in particular, has evolved into more than just a digital resume or networking site; it's now a powerful tool for personal branding. Recruiters use LinkedIn not only to search for potential candidates but also to evaluate a person's professional presence. A complete, well-maintained LinkedIn profile can serve as an online portfolio that highlights your skills, achievements, and connections. Beyond your resume, recruiters are looking for endorsements, recommendations, and evidence of your professional network.

In addition to job search platforms, social media plays an increasingly important role in the hiring process. Employers often review a candidate's social media presence, from LinkedIn to Twitter, Facebook, and Instagram. Job seekers who carefully curate their social media profiles can leverage them to reflect their personal and professional brand. Conversely, a negative online presence can quickly disqualify an otherwise strong candidate.

The explosion of online platforms has also shifted power dynamics in the job search process. Sites like Glassdoor allow candidates to leave reviews of companies and interview experiences, which can either bolster or tarnish a company's reputation. Job seekers are now more informed than ever before, with access to insider knowledge about company culture, salary ranges, and interview processes. While this transparency benefits candidates, it also means that companies need to invest in their employer brand, ensuring that they are perceived as attractive places to work.

Globalization and Remote Work

Globalization has dramatically altered the job market, making it more competitive and interconnected than ever before. Thanks to advances in technology, companies can now hire talent from around the world, and remote work has become a norm for many industries, especially after the COVID-19 pandemic. This shift has widened the talent pool, making it easier for companies to find specialized skills regardless of geographic location. However, it has also increased competition, as job seekers are no longer competing only with local candidates but also with individuals from different countries and time zones.

Remote work has fundamentally changed the hiring process. Virtual interviews, digital onboarding, and remote team management have become common practices, allowing companies to hire talent without the need for physical proximity. While this trend has opened up new opportunities for job seekers, it also requires a different skill set. Candidates must demonstrate that they can work independently, manage their time effectively, and stay productive without direct supervision.

The rise of remote work has also influenced the qualities that employers prioritize. Soft skills such as communication, collaboration, and adaptability have become even more important, as remote workers need to navigate virtual communication tools and maintain strong working relationships without face-to-face interaction. Additionally, the ability to self-motivate and stay organized in a remote environment is now a critical differentiator for candidates.

What Employers Are Really Looking For

While technical skills and experience are still essential, employers today are increasingly looking for a well-rounded candidate who possesses both hard and soft skills. In the past, a person's qualifications on paper might have been enough to secure a job. But today, employers are seeking individuals who can not only do the job but also contribute to the company's culture, adapt to changes, and grow with the organization.

The Importance of Soft Skills

Soft skills—such as communication, teamwork, emotional intelligence, and problem-solving—have become critical components of what employers are looking for. These skills are often the differentiating factor between two candidates with similar qualifications. A recent survey by LinkedIn revealed that 92% of hiring managers believe soft skills are equally or more important than technical skills, yet they are often the hardest to find.

Communication is arguably the most important soft skill in today's job market. Employers need team members who can articulate ideas clearly, whether in writing or in person. With remote work and virtual teams becoming more common, the ability to communicate effectively across digital platforms has become even more vital. Strong communication also extends to listening—employers are looking for individuals who can not only express their thoughts but also listen actively and respond thoughtfully.

Collaboration and teamwork are other highly valued skills. The modern workplace is often project-based and team-oriented, requiring employees to work closely with colleagues from diverse backgrounds and expertise. Employers want to know that you can contribute to a team's success while also managing any conflicts or challenges that arise. Being a team player also means being adaptable and open to feedback, which are qualities that can significantly enhance your chances of standing out in the hiring process.

Emotional intelligence (EQ) has become a buzzword in the hiring world, and for good reason. EQ refers to the ability to understand and manage your own emotions while also recognizing and influencing the emotions of others. In the workplace, this translates to being able to navigate interpersonal relationships, handle stress, and lead with empathy. Employers are increasingly looking for candidates who demonstrate emotional intelligence, as it's a key factor in building strong teams and maintaining a positive work environment.

Problem-solving and critical thinking are other top skills that employers value. In a rapidly changing business landscape, companies need employees who can think on their feet, analyze complex situations, and come up with creative solutions. Employers want to see that you can not only identify problems but also take initiative to solve them, often with limited resources or guidance.

Adaptability and Learning Agility

The pace of technological and economic change means that companies need employees who are adaptable and willing to learn new skills. Adaptability is about being able to adjust to new circumstances, embrace change, and remain effective in uncertain environments. Whether it's learning a new software tool, adapting to remote work, or taking on new responsibilities, employers are looking for candidates who can pivot when necessary and maintain a positive attitude throughout.

Learning agility—the ability to quickly pick up new skills and apply them in different contexts—is increasingly important in today's job market. In many industries, the skills required today may be outdated in a few years, so employers are seeking candidates who are committed to continuous learning. This might mean upskilling through online courses, attending industry conferences, or simply staying up-to-date with the latest trends and developments in your field.

In interviews, demonstrating your adaptability and learning agility can set you apart. For example, you might share a story about a time when you had to quickly learn a new skill or adapt to a major change in your role. By showing that you're comfortable with change and eager to learn, you'll position yourself as a forward-thinking candidate who can thrive in today's fast-paced work environment.

CHAPTER 1: UNDERSTANDING THE MODERN JOB MARKET

The modern job market is complex, fast-paced, and constantly evolving. Understanding the current trends in hiring practices, as well as what employers are truly looking for, is essential for job seekers who want to stand out. Whether it's navigating AI-powered recruitment tools, building a strong online presence, or honing in-demand soft skills, adapting to the new realities of the job market can make all the difference in landing your dream job. As companies continue to embrace technology and global talent, the most successful candidates will be those who can balance technical expertise with emotional intelligence, collaboration, and a willingness to learn.

Chapter 2: Crafting a Stand-Out Resume

In today's competitive job market, a resume is much more than just a list of your work history and qualifications—it's a personal marketing tool. It serves as the first impression you give to potential employers, and in many cases, it's the key that opens the door to an interview. To truly stand out, you need to go beyond the basics of listing your job experiences. You must craft a resume that speaks directly to the job you're applying for, showcases your achievements in a quantifiable way, and is designed with readability and impact in mind.

Tailoring Your Resume to Each Job

One of the biggest mistakes job seekers make is sending out a one-size-fits-all resume. While it may seem efficient to have a single resume that you send to multiple employers, the truth is that this approach can often backfire. Recruiters and hiring managers are looking for candidates who align closely with the job description, and if your resume doesn't clearly demonstrate that you're a perfect fit, you may be passed over. Tailoring your resume to each specific job posting is crucial if you want to stand out from the competition.

Understanding the Job Description

The first step in tailoring your resume is to carefully analyze the job description. Employers often use job descriptions to list the qualifications, skills, and experiences they deem most important for the role. Pay close attention to the keywords used in the description—these are often the same keywords that Applicant Tracking Systems (ATS) and recruiters will be looking for in your resume. ATS software is designed to scan resumes for these keywords, filtering out candidates who don't seem like a good match based on their alignment with the job posting.

For example, if a job description emphasizes "project management," "data analysis," and "leadership," those terms should appear in your resume, assuming you possess those skills. However, don't just list these words without providing context. You need to demonstrate how you've successfully used these skills in your previous roles. Highlight specific projects or responsibilities that align with the key requirements of the job.

Customizing Your Resume Sections

When tailoring your resume, think about how each section can be adjusted to better match the job you're applying for. Here are a few strategies:

- **Professional Summary:** The professional summary at the top of your resume should be a concise but powerful snapshot of who you are as a candidate. Instead of writing a generic summary, customize it to reflect the exact role you're applying for. For instance, if the job is for a marketing manager position, your summary should emphasize your marketing expertise, leadership experience, and results-driven mindset.
- **Skills Section:** The skills section is another area where customization is key. Employers often list specific technical and soft skills they are seeking, so be sure to highlight the ones that are most relevant to the position. However, avoid simply copying and pasting the job description into your resume. You want to show that you possess these skills through real-world experience, so focus on including skills that you've demonstrated in past roles.
- **Work Experience:** When listing your work experience, reorder the bullet points to prioritize the responsibilities and achievements that are most relevant to the job you're applying for. If a job description emphasizes leadership and project management, make sure these elements appear prominently in the descriptions of your previous roles. Use language that mirrors the job posting to demonstrate alignment without being repetitive.

- **Education and Certifications:** If the job requires specific educational qualifications or certifications, be sure to emphasize these prominently in your resume. Consider moving this section closer to the top of your resume if your education is particularly relevant to the role.

Tailoring Without Overcomplicating

While it's important to tailor your resume to each job, it's also crucial not to overcomplicate the process. You don't need to completely rewrite your resume for every job application; instead, make smart adjustments that help align your resume more closely with the job posting. By maintaining a strong base resume that includes your key achievements and skills, you can make targeted changes for each job without starting from scratch every time.

Highlighting Your Achievements

A standout resume is one that doesn't just describe what you've done in the past—it showcases what you've accomplished. Hiring managers want to see measurable results that demonstrate your value. Instead of listing responsibilities, focus on highlighting your achievements, backed by quantifiable data wherever possible. This approach helps differentiate you from other candidates and provides concrete evidence of your contributions.

Quantifying Your Accomplishments

One of the best ways to highlight your achievements is by using numbers. Quantifying your accomplishments not only makes them more tangible but also gives hiring managers a clearer understanding of the impact you've had in previous roles. When describing your achievements, ask yourself how you can express the results in terms of numbers, percentages, or time frames.

For example, instead of writing, "Managed a sales team," a more compelling version would be: "Managed a sales team of 10, leading to a 15% increase in revenue over 12 months." This provides specific, measurable evidence of your leadership and the positive outcomes of your work.

Here are some ways to quantify your achievements:

- **Revenue Increases:** If you were involved in generating revenue, be specific about the numbers. "Increased company revenue by 20% in the first quarter through targeted marketing campaigns" is much more impactful than simply saying, "Improved company revenue."
- **Cost Savings:** If your efforts resulted in cost savings for your company, mention how much was saved and over what period. For instance, "Reduced operational costs by 30% annually by implementing new supply chain strategies."
- **Efficiency Improvements:** If you streamlined processes or improved efficiency, quantify the time saved or the reduction in resources needed. For example, "Cut project delivery time by 25% by implementing agile project management techniques."
- **Team Leadership:** If you managed a team or played a leadership role, include information about the size of the team and the outcomes achieved under your leadership. For example, "Led a team of 15 in the successful launch of a new product, generating $500,000 in sales in the first three months."

Using Action Verbs

When describing your achievements, use strong action verbs that convey leadership, initiative, and results. Words like "increased," "led," "generated," "improved," and "optimized" show that you were proactive in your role and contributed to meaningful outcomes. Passive language, on the other hand, can make it sound like you were merely following instructions without taking initiative. By using action-oriented language, you can paint a picture of yourself as a results-driven professional who adds value to the organizations you work for.

Framing Your Achievements in the STAR Format

One effective way to structure your achievements on your resume is by using the STAR method, which stands for Situation, Task, Action, and Result. This framework helps you to provide context around your accomplishments and to showcase not only what you achieved but how you achieved it.

- **Situation:** Describe the context or challenge you faced.
- **Task:** Explain the goal or responsibility you were assigned.
- **Action:** Detail the specific steps you took to address the challenge or task.
- **Result:** Highlight the outcome, ideally with quantifiable data.

For example:

- Situation: "The company was facing declining customer retention rates."
- Task: "I was tasked with designing and implementing a new customer loyalty program."
- Action: "I conducted customer surveys to understand pain points and collaborated with the marketing team to create targeted offers."
- Result: "The program increased customer retention by 20% within six months."

Using the STAR method ensures that your achievements are not just a list of actions but well-rounded examples of your ability to deliver results.

Designing for Readability and Impact

In addition to the content of your resume, the design and formatting are critical to making a strong impression. A well-designed resume is one that's easy to read, aesthetically appealing, and strategically structured to draw attention to your most important qualifications and achievements.

Prioritizing Readability

One of the primary goals of resume design is readability. Recruiters often spend only a few seconds reviewing each resume, so it's essential that your key information is easy to find and digest. Here are some tips for improving readability:

- **Use a Clean, Simple Layout:** Avoid overly complicated designs that may distract from the content. Stick to a clean, professional layout with clearly defined sections and plenty of white space. This makes your resume easier to scan quickly.

- **Choose a Professional Font:** Select a simple, professional font such as Arial, Calibri, or Times New Roman. Avoid using decorative fonts, as they can make your resume harder to read and may not be taken seriously in a professional setting.
- **Use Bullet Points:** Bullet points make it easier for recruiters to scan through your achievements and responsibilities. Each bullet should be a concise, impactful statement that highlights a key aspect of your experience or skills.
- **Maintain Consistent Formatting:** Ensure that the formatting of your resume is consistent throughout. For example, if you bold the job titles in one section, make sure all job titles are bolded. Consistency in formatting helps create a polished, professional appearance.

Creating Visual Impact

While readability is paramount, you also want your resume to have a strong visual impact. A visually appealing resume will grab the recruiter's attention and make it more likely that they'll spend time reviewing your qualifications. Here are some strategies for enhancing the visual appeal of your resume:

- **Use a Two-Column Layout:** A two-column layout can help you make better use of space and highlight important information in a visually appealing way. For example, you could list your contact information, skills, and certifications in one column, while using the other column for your work experience and achievements.
- **Incorporate Subheadings and Section Breaks:** Clearly defined subheadings and section breaks help guide the reader's eye through your resume. Use bold or slightly larger text for section titles such as "Work Experience," "Education," and "Skills."
- **Use Color Strategically:** A touch of color can help your resume stand out, but it's important to use color sparingly and strategically. Stick to professional colors such as navy blue, dark gray, or burgundy for section

headings or borders.
- **Use Icons for Key Sections:** Adding small, professional icons next to section headings (e.g., an education icon next to the "Education" section) can add a visual cue that makes your resume more engaging. However, make sure these elements are subtle and don't distract from the content.

Crafting a standout resume is about more than just listing your job history. It's about creating a tailored, results-driven document that highlights your achievements and aligns with the specific job you're applying for. By customizing your resume for each job, showcasing measurable results, and designing it for readability and impact, you'll be well on your way to creating a resume that not only gets noticed but also sets you apart from the competition.

Chapter 3: Perfecting the Cover Letter

A well-crafted cover letter can make all the difference when it comes to standing out in the hiring process. While your resume lists your qualifications and accomplishments, the cover letter allows you to make a more personal connection with the hiring manager and offer deeper insights into who you are as a candidate. It's your opportunity to explain why you're not only qualified for the position but also passionate about the company and the role. Despite its importance, many candidates overlook the cover letter or see it as a formality, which can be a huge missed opportunity.

In this chapter, we'll explore how to write a compelling cover letter that helps you stand out, the common pitfalls to avoid, and how to effectively tell your story in a way that positions you as the perfect fit for the job.

Making a Personal Connection

One of the key purposes of a cover letter is to create a personal connection with the person reading it. A generic, one-size-fits-all letter will fail to resonate with hiring managers, but a personalized cover letter can help you build rapport and show that you're genuinely interested in the role.

Addressing the Hiring Manager by Name

One of the simplest and most effective ways to make your cover letter feel personal is by addressing the hiring manager by name. Instead of using the impersonal "To Whom It May Concern" or "Dear Hiring Manager," take the time to find out the name of the person who will be reviewing your application. This small detail shows that you've done your homework and are genuinely interested in the position.

There are several ways to find the hiring manager's name. Start by looking at the job posting itself—sometimes, the contact information is listed there. If not, you can check the company's website, look at LinkedIn profiles of employees in the department you're applying to, or call the company's HR department and ask directly. Even if you can't find the exact name, making an effort to address the letter to a specific role or team (e.g., "Dear Marketing Team" or "Dear Sales Director") is better than using a generic greeting.

Connecting Your Experience with the Company's Needs

A cover letter isn't just about explaining why you're qualified—it's about explaining why you're the perfect fit for the company. To do this, you need to show that you understand the company's mission, goals, and challenges, and then explain how your background and skills can help address them. The more specific you can be, the more likely you are to grab the hiring manager's attention.

Before you start writing, do your research on the company. Look at their website, read recent press releases, and browse their social media channels to get a sense of their culture and priorities. What are their current goals? Are they launching a new product, expanding into a new market, or trying to solve a particular problem? Use this information to frame your cover letter in a way that connects your experience with their needs.

For example, if you're applying for a marketing position and you see that the company is focused on increasing its digital presence, you might say something like: "I was particularly excited to see that [Company Name] is focused on expanding its digital marketing efforts. In my previous role, I helped increase website traffic by 30% through targeted social media campaigns and SEO optimization, and I would love to bring that experience to your team as you continue to grow."

By tying your experience to the company's goals, you demonstrate that you're not only qualified but also invested in helping the company succeed.

Showcasing Passion and Enthusiasm

Hiring managers are looking for more than just qualifications—they want to hire someone who is passionate about the role and excited about the

CHAPTER 3: PERFECTING THE COVER LETTER

opportunity to work for their company. Enthusiasm can often be the deciding factor between two equally qualified candidates, so don't be afraid to show it in your cover letter.

This doesn't mean that you should go overboard with flattery or use clichés like "I've always dreamed of working for your company." Instead, focus on explaining why this particular role excites you and how it aligns with your long-term career goals. For example, you might say: "I've always been passionate about using technology to solve real-world problems, which is why I was thrilled to learn about this opportunity at [Company Name]. Your focus on innovative, customer-centric solutions aligns perfectly with my experience and career aspirations."

Showing genuine enthusiasm can help you stand out as a candidate who isn't just looking for any job, but is specifically interested in this job at this company.

Avoiding Common Pitfalls

While a well-written cover letter can make a positive impression, a poorly crafted one can do just the opposite. There are several common pitfalls that candidates often fall into when writing cover letters, and avoiding these can significantly increase your chances of success.

Being Too Generic

One of the most common mistakes candidates make is sending out a generic cover letter that could apply to any job. Hiring managers can easily spot a template letter, and it sends the message that you're not particularly interested in their company. A generic letter doesn't tell the hiring manager anything about why you're a good fit for the role or why you want to work for their organization.

Instead of using a one-size-fits-all approach, take the time to customize each cover letter for the specific job and company. This doesn't mean you need to start from scratch every time—having a strong base cover letter is fine—but you should tailor each letter to reflect the company's needs and the specific requirements of the role.

Focusing Too Much on Yourself

While it's important to highlight your qualifications and achievements, your cover letter should ultimately be about how you can help the company. A cover letter that focuses solely on what you want out of the job ("I'm looking for opportunities to grow," "I want to gain more experience in this field") can come across as self-centered and may not resonate with hiring managers.

Instead, focus on what you can offer the company. How can your skills, experience, and knowledge contribute to their success? By shifting the focus from what you want to what you can provide, you position yourself as a valuable asset to the organization.

Repeating Your Resume

Another common pitfall is simply rehashing the content of your resume in the cover letter. While your resume lists your qualifications, your cover letter should offer deeper insights into how those qualifications make you a good fit for the job. Instead of listing your previous job titles and responsibilities, use your cover letter to explain the context behind your experience and how it has prepared you for this role.

For example, rather than writing: "I have five years of experience in customer service," you could say: "In my five years of experience in customer service, I have developed strong communication and problem-solving skills, which I used to consistently exceed customer satisfaction goals. I am excited to bring this expertise to your team and help [Company Name] continue to deliver exceptional customer experiences."

By offering more context and insight, you can make your cover letter more engaging and impactful.

Making It Too Long

Hiring managers are busy, and they don't have time to read a long, rambling cover letter. Ideally, your cover letter should be no longer than one page and should get straight to the point. Avoid including irrelevant information or going into too much detail about your entire career history. Instead, focus on the key points that are most relevant to the job you're applying for.

Keep your writing clear, concise, and focused on demonstrating why you're the best candidate for the position.

Using Clichés and Overly Formal Language

It's easy to fall into the trap of using clichés and overly formal language in a cover letter, especially if you're unsure of what to say. Phrases like "I'm a hard worker" or "I have a proven track record of success" don't add much value and can make your letter sound generic.

Instead of relying on clichés, be specific about what makes you a great candidate. Use clear, straightforward language to explain how your skills and experience align with the company's needs.

Telling Your Story Effectively

One of the most powerful ways to stand out in your cover letter is by telling your story. Rather than simply listing your qualifications, use your cover letter to weave a narrative that connects your background, experiences, and career goals to the role you're applying for. A compelling story can make you more memorable and help the hiring manager see you as a unique candidate who is not only qualified but also motivated and driven.

Starting with a Strong Hook

Your cover letter should grab the reader's attention from the very first sentence. Instead of starting with a generic introduction like "I'm writing to apply for the position of…," consider opening with a strong hook that immediately draws the reader in.

For example, you might start by mentioning a recent project or accomplishment that's relevant to the job: "As a digital marketing specialist who recently led a successful campaign that increased web traffic by 40%, I was excited to see the opening at [Company Name]." This type of opening immediately demonstrates your value and piques the reader's interest.

Another approach is to mention a personal connection to the company or its mission: "Having been a long-time admirer of [Company Name]'s commitment to sustainability, I was thrilled to see an opening for a product manager role that would allow me to contribute to your efforts in reducing environmental impact."

A strong hook sets the tone for the rest of the letter and encourages the hiring manager to keep reading.

Connecting the Dots Between Your Experience and the Role

Once you've grabbed the reader's attention, the next step is to connect the dots between your experience and the job you're applying for. Use your cover letter to explain how your background has prepared you for the specific challenges and responsibilities of the role.

For example, if you're applying for a project management position, you might say: "In my previous role, I managed cross-functional teams on a variety of complex projects, consistently delivering results on time and under budget. I'm confident that my ability to coordinate teams, manage resources, and communicate effectively would make me a valuable asset to your project management team."

By clearly linking your experience to the job requirements, you show the hiring manager that you understand the role and are equipped to succeed in it.

Demonstrating Your Unique Value

Every candidate has a unique combination of skills, experience, and personality that sets them apart from others. Your cover letter is your chance to highlight what makes you different and why you're the best fit for the job.

Ask yourself: What specific skills or experiences do you bring to the table that other candidates might not? How can you contribute to the company in ways that go beyond the basic job description?

For example, if you have experience working in a particular industry or have a unique skill set that's relevant to the role, be sure to mention it: "With my background in both graphic design and front-end development, I bring a unique perspective to UX design that allows me to create visually compelling and highly functional interfaces."

By demonstrating your unique value, you set yourself apart from other candidates and show the hiring manager why you're the best choice for the role.

CHAPTER 3: PERFECTING THE COVER LETTER

A well-crafted cover letter can be the key to standing out in a crowded job market. By making a personal connection, avoiding common pitfalls, and telling your story effectively, you can create a cover letter that not only gets noticed but also positions you as the perfect fit for the job. Remember, your cover letter is your chance to showcase your personality, passion, and unique value—so make the most of it and let your true self shine through.

Chapter 4: Researching the Company and Industry

Walking into an interview prepared with in-depth knowledge about the company and its industry not only sets you apart as a serious candidate but also gives you a competitive edge. In today's job market, where hundreds of applicants may be vying for the same role, understanding the company's culture, the industry's trends, and even connecting with current employees can help you position yourself as a strong candidate who's well-prepared and genuinely interested. Employers value candidates who take the time to do their homework, as it shows dedication, initiative, and a strong desire to succeed within the organization.

In this chapter, we'll explore how to effectively research the company you're applying to, from digging into their culture to understanding the broader industry landscape. We'll also look at how networking with current employees can provide invaluable insights that can enhance your interview performance.

Digging into Company Culture

Understanding a company's culture is essential when preparing for an interview. Company culture reflects the organization's values, mission, work environment, and the overall employee experience. Companies want to hire people who not only have the right skills but who will also fit in with their culture and contribute positively to the team dynamic. Researching company culture helps you tailor your interview responses to show how your values and work style align with those of the company.

Using Glassdoor to Gain Insights

One of the most popular resources for researching company culture is Glassdoor. This platform allows current and former employees to leave reviews about their experiences working at a company, providing valuable insights into the company's work environment, management style, and overall employee satisfaction.

When using Glassdoor, pay attention to recurring themes in the reviews. Are employees generally happy with the company's leadership and direction? Do they feel supported in their professional growth? What are the company's strengths and weaknesses? While individual reviews can sometimes be biased or overly negative, patterns in the feedback can help you identify common aspects of the company's culture. For example, if multiple employees mention that the company encourages work-life balance, you can emphasize in your interview how you value a healthy balance and thrive in environments that support it.

Additionally, Glassdoor provides insights into company benefits, salary expectations, and even potential interview questions. By reviewing the interview section, you can get a sense of what types of questions the company tends to ask and what they prioritize in candidates, helping you prepare more effectively.

Exploring LinkedIn for Cultural Clues

LinkedIn is another excellent tool for learning about company culture. While LinkedIn is primarily a professional networking platform, it also provides a window into how a company presents itself to the world. Start by visiting the company's LinkedIn page and reviewing its posts, articles, and updates. Pay attention to the language they use and the type of content they share. Are they highlighting employee achievements? Showcasing community involvement or sustainability initiatives? Sharing thought leadership in their industry? All of these factors can give you insights into the company's values and what they prioritize.

You can also look at the profiles of current employees to get a sense of the type of professionals who work there. Do they share common skills, experiences, or values? How long do employees typically stay with the company? What types of endorsements or recommendations do they receive? By reviewing employees' profiles, you can better understand the company's expectations and what qualities are valued in its workforce.

Analyzing the Company's Website and Social Media

A company's website and social media presence are key sources of information about its culture. The "About Us" or "Careers" sections of a company's website often provide direct insights into its values, mission statement, and organizational goals. Read the company's mission statement carefully to understand what drives their operations and what they seek to achieve in their industry. Additionally, look for information about the company's community involvement, sustainability efforts, and employee programs—these can give you a clear idea of how the company supports its workforce and what causes they care about.

On social media platforms like Twitter, Facebook, and Instagram, companies often share real-time updates, employee spotlights, and glimpses into day-to-day operations. By following the company's social media pages, you can gain a deeper understanding of their workplace culture and what it might be like to work there. Social media also reveals how the company interacts with its customers and the general public, which can be valuable information during an interview.

For example, if a company frequently posts about diversity and inclusion initiatives, you might want to highlight your own experiences or values related to those topics in the interview. If the company values creativity and innovation, you could mention times when you've brought fresh ideas to the table in your previous roles.

Understanding Industry Trends

In addition to understanding the specific company, it's essential to stay informed about the broader industry in which the company operates. Industry knowledge demonstrates that you're not only focused on the position at hand but also understand the challenges and opportunities the company may face in its sector. Being knowledgeable about the latest industry trends allows you to ask insightful questions during the interview and present yourself as a well-informed candidate.

Identifying Key Trends in the Industry

To stay updated on industry trends, start by reading relevant industry publications, blogs, and reports. There are numerous online resources available for almost every industry, from technology and finance to healthcare and marketing. Websites like Harvard Business Review, Forbes, and industry-specific publications (e.g., TechCrunch for tech or Adweek for advertising) provide valuable insights into the latest developments, challenges, and innovations.

You can also subscribe to newsletters or follow thought leaders on LinkedIn who frequently share updates and insights about your target industry. Thought leaders often provide commentary on emerging trends, new technologies, and changes in the competitive landscape, giving you a broader perspective on the industry.

When you're informed about the latest trends, you can better tailor your interview responses to show that you understand the current state of the industry and how it might affect the company. For example, if you're interviewing for a role in retail and you're aware that e-commerce is rapidly growing, you could talk about your experience with digital marketing or online sales and how you can help the company expand its e-commerce presence.

Discussing Industry Trends in the Interview

Once you've identified key trends, think about how they relate to the company you're interviewing with. Are there any recent developments that could impact the company's operations or strategy? For example, if you're interviewing for a role at a financial services firm, you might want to bring up the rise of fintech and how it's disrupting traditional banking models. By demonstrating that you're aware of these trends, you position yourself as a candidate who thinks strategically and is prepared to help the company navigate industry changes.

During the interview, you can also ask questions that show your knowledge of industry trends. For example, you might ask: "How is the company adapting to the increasing importance of [trend]?" or "What role do you see [emerging technology] playing in the future of your industry?" These questions not only demonstrate your knowledge but also show that you're thinking critically about the company's future.

Networking with Current Employees

While researching a company's website and using tools like Glassdoor and LinkedIn can provide valuable information, nothing beats firsthand insights from people who currently work at the company. Networking with current employees can give you a more accurate picture of the company's culture, expectations, and challenges—and it can also help you stand out during the interview process.

The Power of Informational Interviews

One of the most effective ways to connect with current employees is by conducting informational interviews. An informational interview is a casual conversation where you can ask questions about the company, the role, and the industry. It's not a job interview, so there's no pressure on either side—it's simply an opportunity to gather information.

To set up an informational interview, start by identifying people within the company who work in the department or role you're interested in. You can use LinkedIn to find employees and reach out with a polite, personalized message. For example, you might say: "Hi [Name], I came across your profile and saw that you work at [Company]. I'm very interested in learning more about the company and the [specific role], and I would love to hear about your experience. Would you be open to a brief conversation?"

If the person agrees, come prepared with thoughtful questions. Ask about the company culture, the team dynamics, and what it's like to work in the role you're applying for. You can also ask for advice on the interview process and how to best position yourself as a candidate. By showing genuine interest and curiosity, you build a rapport with the employee, who may even put in a good word for you with the hiring manager.

Building Connections Through LinkedIn

LinkedIn is an excellent platform for networking with current employees. In addition to informational interviews, you can engage with employees by commenting on their posts or articles. This shows that you're not only following the company but also engaging with its employees and staying up to date with its activities.

When reaching out to connect on LinkedIn, make sure to personalize your connection request. Mention something specific about their background, the company, or a recent post they shared. A personalized message is much more likely to get a response than a generic request.

For example, you might say: "Hi [Name], I noticed that you recently shared an article about [topic], which I found really insightful. I'm currently exploring opportunities at [Company], and I'd love to connect and learn more about your experience there."

By taking the time to build relationships with employees, you not only gain valuable insights but also increase your visibility within the company. In some cases, employees may even refer you for the role, which can significantly improve your chances of getting an interview.

Navigating Company Events and Webinars

Many companies host public events, webinars, or conferences where potential candidates can learn more about the company and its industry. Attending these events can provide valuable networking opportunities and allow you to hear directly from company leaders and employees.

These events can be a goldmine for gathering information and establishing connections.

Maximizing Networking Opportunities at Events

When attending a company event or webinar, come prepared with questions to ask speakers or panelists. This not only demonstrates your interest but also positions you as someone who is engaged and knowledgeable. For example, you might ask a panelist about the company's approach to a specific industry challenge or how they envision the future of the industry evolving. Engaging in meaningful conversations can lead to further connections and insights.

Don't forget to network with other attendees as well. Fellow job seekers can provide valuable information about their experiences and insights regarding the company. After the event, consider following up with anyone you spoke to on LinkedIn, mentioning your conversation and expressing interest in staying connected.

Putting It All Together: Researching for the Interview

Now that you have a solid understanding of how to research the company and its industry, it's time to put this knowledge into action. Here's a step-by-step guide to effectively prepare for your interview by researching the company and industry:

1. **Identify Key Resources:**

- Start with the company's website, Glassdoor, and LinkedIn. Make notes on the company's mission, values, and any employee reviews that stand out.
- Look for industry publications and blogs to gather insights into current trends that might impact the company.

1. **Analyze Company Culture:**

- Reflect on what you've learned about the company's culture from employee reviews and social media. Consider how your values align with those of the company.
- Identify specific examples from your own experience that demonstrate how you fit into their culture.

1. **Stay Informed About Industry Trends:**

- Create a list of recent developments or trends within the industry that

you can reference during the interview.
- Think about how these trends relate to the role you're applying for and how you can contribute to the company's goals in this context.

1. **Network with Current Employees:**

- Reach out to current employees for informational interviews to gather firsthand insights.
- Prepare thoughtful questions to ask, focusing on the company culture, team dynamics, and potential challenges the company may face.

1. **Prepare Questions for the Interview:**

- Based on your research, come up with insightful questions to ask the interviewer about the company, its culture, and how it adapts to industry changes.
- Show that you're informed and interested in not just the role but the organization as a whole.

1. **Practice Your Responses:**

- Incorporate your research into your interview responses. Highlight how your skills and experiences align with the company's values and the current industry landscape.
- Be ready to discuss industry trends and how they may affect the company in the future, demonstrating your strategic thinking and interest.

In today's competitive job market, simply applying for a position is not enough. Researching the company and its industry is crucial to standing out from the crowd and demonstrating your commitment to being the best candidate for the role. By digging into company culture, understanding industry trends, and networking with current employees, you position yourself as a well-informed and engaged candidate.

Your thorough research will not only prepare you to answer questions more effectively but will also equip you with the knowledge to ask insightful questions that demonstrate your genuine interest in the company and its future. As you prepare for your interview, remember that knowledge is power, and the more you know about the company and its industry, the better equipped you will be to ace your interview and make a lasting impression.

Chapter 5: Preparing for Common Interview Questions

As the saying goes, "Failing to prepare is preparing to fail." This rings especially true when it comes to job interviews. One of the most effective ways to prepare is to understand the types of questions you're likely to encounter and develop a strategy for answering them effectively. In this chapter, we'll explore the distinction between behavioral and situational questions, introduce the STAR method to help structure your answers, and discuss how to master the "Tell Me About Yourself" question to make a strong first impression.

Behavioral vs. Situational Questions

When preparing for an interview, it's essential to understand the two main types of questions you might face: behavioral and situational. Each type serves a different purpose and requires a different approach.

Behavioral Questions

Behavioral questions are based on the premise that past behavior is the best predictor of future performance. These questions often begin with phrases like "Tell me about a time when…" or "Give me an example of…" and require you to draw upon your previous experiences to illustrate your skills and competencies. Employers use behavioral questions to assess how you handle challenges, work with others, and navigate various situations in the workplace.

For example, a typical behavioral question might be: "Can you describe a situation where you had to deal with a difficult team member? What did you do, and what was the outcome?" To answer this type of question effectively, you need to provide a specific example from your past that demonstrates your abilities and problem-solving skills.

Situational Questions

In contrast, situational questions are hypothetical and focus on how you would handle a specific situation in the future. These questions often start with phrases like "What would you do if…" or "How would you handle…" Employers use situational questions to evaluate your critical thinking skills, problem-solving abilities, and how well you align with the company's values and expectations.

An example of a situational question might be: "If you were assigned a project with a tight deadline and you realized that your team was behind schedule, what steps would you take to get back on track?" In this case, the interviewer wants to understand your thought process and how you would approach the situation.

Strategies for Answering Both Types of Questions

To prepare for both behavioral and situational questions, consider the following strategies:

1. **Reflect on Past Experiences:** For behavioral questions, think about specific situations from your past work experiences that highlight your skills and abilities. Consider challenges you've faced, how you approached them, and the outcomes.
2. **Practice Hypothetical Scenarios:** For situational questions, practice thinking through various scenarios that could occur in the workplace. Think about the skills and strategies you would employ to resolve these situations.
3. **Use a Mix of Examples:** When answering questions, draw upon both behavioral and situational examples. This not only showcases your past experiences but also demonstrates your ability to think critically and problem-solve in hypothetical situations.

4. **Align Your Answers with Company Values:** Always relate your responses back to the company's values and culture. This shows that you understand what the organization prioritizes and that you're capable of contributing positively to its goals.

The STAR Method for Success

One of the most effective techniques for answering behavioral questions is the STAR method. The STAR method provides a structured way to respond to questions by breaking your answer into four key components: Situation, Task, Action, and Result. This method allows you to present your experiences in a clear, concise manner, highlighting your skills and competencies effectively.

Breaking Down the STAR Method

1. **Situation:** Start by setting the scene and providing context for your story. Describe the situation you were in and any relevant background information that helps the interviewer understand the circumstances.
2. *Example:* "In my previous role as a marketing coordinator, we faced a challenge when our website traffic dropped significantly during a critical campaign. This was concerning, as we relied heavily on online leads to meet our sales goals."
3. **Task:** Next, explain your specific responsibilities and what was required of you in that situation. Be clear about your role and the objectives you were aiming to achieve.
4. *Example:* "As the marketing lead for the campaign, my task was to identify the cause of the drop in traffic and develop a strategy to increase our online visibility and lead generation."
5. **Action:** This is where you outline the steps you took to address the situation. Focus on the actions you specifically took, rather than what the team or organization did as a whole.
6. *Example:* "I conducted an analysis of our website and identified several technical issues that were impacting our search engine rankings. I worked closely with our IT team to resolve these issues and implemented

a targeted social media advertising strategy to drive traffic back to the site."
7. **Result:** Finally, share the outcomes of your actions. Highlight any measurable results, positive feedback, or lessons learned from the experience.
8. *Example:* "As a result of my efforts, we saw a 30% increase in website traffic within two weeks, leading to a significant boost in leads generated from our campaign. The management team praised our quick turnaround, and I learned valuable lessons about the importance of monitoring performance metrics closely."

By structuring your answers using the STAR method, you can effectively communicate your experiences while demonstrating your problem-solving abilities and competence.

Nailing the "Tell Me About Yourself" Question

One of the most common opening questions in any interview is, "Tell me about yourself." While this question may seem simple, it can often set the tone for the rest of the interview. It's your opportunity to make a strong first impression and showcase your qualifications, experiences, and personality.

Crafting Your Response

When answering the "Tell Me About Yourself" question, consider the following steps to create a compelling response:

1. **Start with a Strong Opening:** Begin with a brief introduction that includes your name and a summary of your professional background. This sets the stage for your response and provides the interviewer with context.
2. *Example:* "Sure! My name is Sarah, and I'm a marketing professional with over five years of experience in digital marketing and content creation."
3. **Highlight Relevant Experience:** Provide a concise overview of your key qualifications and experiences that are directly relevant to

the position you're applying for. Focus on your most impressive achievements and skills that align with the job description.
4. *Example:* "In my previous role at XYZ Company, I led a team that developed a highly successful social media campaign that increased our brand's online presence by 40% and significantly boosted engagement rates."
5. **Connect to the Job Opportunity:** Show the interviewer why you're interested in the position and how your experiences make you a strong fit for the role. This helps demonstrate your motivation and enthusiasm.
6. *Example:* "I'm particularly excited about this opportunity with ABC Company because I admire your innovative approach to marketing, and I believe my background in data-driven campaigns would allow me to contribute effectively to your team."
7. **Wrap Up with a Personal Touch:** End your response by adding a brief personal touch. This could be a statement about your career aspirations or a mention of your interests outside of work.
8. *Example:* "Outside of work, I'm passionate about photography, which has honed my eye for detail and creativity. I'm excited to bring that perspective to my professional work as well."

Practice Makes Perfect

Practicing your response to the "Tell Me About Yourself" question is crucial. Aim to keep your answer within two to three minutes, ensuring you provide enough detail without overwhelming the interviewer. Rehearse your response until it feels natural and confident.

Consider conducting mock interviews with friends, family, or mentors. Request feedback on your delivery and content, and make adjustments as necessary. The goal is to create a compelling narrative that highlights your qualifications while showcasing your personality.

Preparing for common interview questions is a critical step in your job search journey. Understanding the difference between behavioral and situational questions allows you to tailor your responses effectively, while the STAR method provides a structured approach to showcase your experiences and competencies. Additionally, mastering the "Tell Me About Yourself" question helps you create a strong first impression and set the tone for a successful interview.

By investing time in preparation and practice, you can approach your interviews with confidence, ready to demonstrate your qualifications and make a lasting impact on potential employers. Remember, interviews are not just about answering questions; they are an opportunity to tell your story and showcase why you are the ideal candidate for the job. With the right preparation, you can ace your interviews and move closer to achieving your career goals.

Chapter 6: Mastering the Art of Non-Verbal Communication

In the realm of job interviews, non-verbal communication often speaks louder than words. While your verbal responses are essential in conveying your skills and qualifications, your body language, appearance, and ability to read others can significantly impact the interviewer's perception of you. In this chapter, we will explore the crucial elements of non-verbal communication, including body language cues, the significance of appearance, and strategies for interpreting the interviewer's non-verbal signals.

Body Language Cues

Your body language can convey confidence, enthusiasm, and professionalism—or, conversely, insecurity and disinterest. Understanding how to use body language effectively can enhance your overall presentation during an interview.

Posture

Posture is one of the first things an interviewer notices. A strong, open posture communicates confidence and self-assurance, while a closed or slouched posture can suggest insecurity or a lack of interest.

- **Maintain an Open Posture:** Sit up straight with your shoulders back and arms relaxed at your sides or resting gently on your lap.

Avoid crossing your arms, as this can create a barrier and signal defensiveness. An open posture invites engagement and shows that you are approachable.

- **Lean In Slightly:** When the interviewer is speaking, lean in slightly to show you are engaged and interested in what they have to say. This small adjustment can demonstrate active listening and a genuine interest in the conversation.
- **Avoid Fidgeting:** Nervous habits like tapping your foot, playing with your hair, or repeatedly adjusting your clothing can be distracting and signal anxiety. Practice maintaining stillness and composure to convey confidence.

Gestures

Gestures can enhance your verbal communication and help emphasize your points. However, they should be used judiciously to avoid distractions.

- **Use Purposeful Gestures:** Use hand gestures to illustrate your points and convey enthusiasm. For example, when discussing a significant achievement, you might gesture to highlight key accomplishments. Purposeful gestures can help you appear more dynamic and engaged.
- **Avoid Overdoing It:** While gestures can be beneficial, excessive movement can be distracting. Be mindful of your gestures and aim for a balance that enhances your message without overwhelming your audience.
- **Match Your Gestures to Your Words:** Ensure that your hand movements align with the tone of your speech. If you are discussing something serious, your gestures should be more subdued, whereas a more enthusiastic topic may call for more animated gestures.

Eye Contact

Eye contact is a powerful tool for building rapport and demonstrating confidence. It signals that you are engaged and attentive.

- **Maintain Appropriate Eye Contact:** Strive for consistent eye contact

throughout the interview, especially when responding to questions. This indicates confidence and helps create a connection with the interviewer. Aim to maintain eye contact about 60-70% of the time during the conversation.
- **Avoid Staring:** While eye contact is essential, be mindful not to stare, as it can make the other person uncomfortable. Instead, practice a natural approach by looking into the interviewer's eyes, then occasionally breaking eye contact to look away briefly, such as at their face or hands.
- **Use Eye Contact to Connect:** When responding to a question, look directly at the interviewer to create a sense of connection. If there are multiple interviewers, engage with each of them by making eye contact as you speak.

What Your Appearance Says About You

Your appearance plays a significant role in forming first impressions during an interview. The way you present yourself can communicate your professionalism, attention to detail, and respect for the opportunity.

Dressing for the Job

Understanding the company culture and industry norms is essential when choosing your outfit for an interview.

- **Research Company Dress Codes:** Before the interview, research the company's dress code. Look for cues on their website, social media profiles, and employee reviews on platforms like Glassdoor. Understanding the company's culture will help you determine the appropriate attire.
- **Dress One Step Above:** A general rule of thumb is to dress one step above the company's typical attire. For instance, if the company has a business casual environment, consider wearing business formal attire. This demonstrates professionalism and respect for the opportunity.
- **Choose Appropriate Colors and Styles:** Colors can convey different messages. For example, blue conveys trust and stability, while black

signifies authority and sophistication. Select colors and styles that align with the image you want to project while remaining comfortable and confident in your outfit.

Grooming and Hygiene

Personal grooming is just as important as your outfit. A polished appearance can significantly enhance your overall impression.

- **Maintain Good Hygiene:** Ensure that you are clean and well-groomed. Pay attention to personal hygiene by showering, brushing your teeth, and using deodorant. Avoid strong fragrances, as they can be overwhelming.
- **Neat Hair and Makeup:** Keep your hair tidy and well-groomed. If you wear makeup, opt for a natural look that complements your features. The goal is to look polished and professional without being overly distracting.
- **Limit Accessories:** Choose accessories that are understated and professional. Avoid loud or flashy jewelry that may divert attention from your qualifications and skills.

Reading the Interviewer's Body Language

In addition to being aware of your own body language, it's crucial to read the interviewer's non-verbal cues. Understanding their body language can help you gauge their reactions and adjust your approach accordingly.

Observing Non-Verbal Signals

Pay close attention to the interviewer's body language throughout the conversation. Here are some common signals to watch for:

- **Facial Expressions:** The interviewer's facial expressions can provide insight into their reactions. A smile or nod can indicate approval or engagement, while furrowed brows or a lack of eye contact may suggest confusion or disinterest.
- **Posture Changes:** Take note of how the interviewer's posture shifts during the interview. If they lean back in their chair with crossed arms,

it may signal defensiveness or disinterest. Conversely, if they lean in and maintain an open posture, they are likely engaged and interested in what you're saying.
- **Nodding:** If the interviewer is nodding while you speak, this is a positive sign. It indicates that they are actively listening and agreeing with your points. Use this feedback to reinforce your message and continue the conversation confidently.

Adjusting Your Approach

Based on the interviewer's body language, be prepared to adapt your communication style. Here's how to respond to their non-verbal cues:

- **Mirror Their Energy:** If the interviewer appears enthusiastic and engaged, respond in kind with a similar level of energy. Conversely, if they seem reserved or formal, tone down your enthusiasm and maintain a more professional demeanor.
- **Pause for Reflection:** If you notice the interviewer appears deep in thought or is taking notes, allow for a moment of silence after your response. This gives them time to process your information and formulate their next question.
- **Ask Clarifying Questions:** If you sense confusion or uncertainty in the interviewer's body language, don't hesitate to ask if they need clarification on any points you've made. This shows that you are attuned to their needs and willing to address any concerns.

Mastering the art of non-verbal communication is a vital component of interview success. Your body language, appearance, and ability to read the interviewer's cues can significantly influence the outcome of your interview. By employing effective body language techniques, dressing appropriately for the company culture, and honing your skills in reading non-verbal signals, you can enhance your overall presence and make a lasting impression.

As you prepare for your next interview, remember that communication is not limited to words alone. The non-verbal signals you send can reinforce your qualifications, convey confidence, and establish a strong connection with the interviewer. With practice and awareness, you can master the art of non-verbal communication and elevate your interview performance to new heights.

Chapter 7: Answering Tough Interview Questions

Navigating the intricate landscape of job interviews often leads to tough questions that challenge your composure and credibility. Among these are inquiries about employment gaps, weaknesses, and salary expectations. While these questions can be daunting, with the right strategies, you can turn them into opportunities to demonstrate your suitability for the role. In this chapter, we will explore effective methods to address these tough questions, ensuring you leave a positive impression on your potential employer.

Dealing with Gaps in Employment

Employment gaps can raise concerns for interviewers, prompting questions about your reliability and commitment. However, how you explain these gaps can either reinforce or undermine your credibility. Here are strategies for effectively addressing career breaks.

Understanding the Concerns

Before diving into your explanation, it's essential to acknowledge why interviewers might be wary of employment gaps. Common concerns include:

- **Skill Erosion:** Employers may fear that a lengthy absence from the workforce could lead to outdated skills.
- **Commitment Issues:** Gaps might raise questions about your dedication

to your career and how reliable you will be in the future.
- **Unexplained Circumstances:** A lack of explanation could lead interviewers to speculate about negative reasons for your absence.

By recognizing these concerns, you can tailor your response to address them head-on.

Crafting Your Narrative

When explaining your employment gap, honesty and transparency are crucial. Here's how to frame your story:

1. **Be Honest, But Strategic:**

- If the gap was due to personal reasons—such as caregiving, health issues, or education—briefly explain the situation without going into too much detail. Focus on what you learned during this period or how it has prepared you for the role.
- For example, you might say, "I took time off to care for a family member, which taught me valuable organizational and multitasking skills that I believe will be beneficial in this position."

1. **Emphasize Continuous Learning:**

- Highlight any relevant activities you engaged in during your time away from the workforce, such as volunteering, taking courses, or pursuing certifications. This demonstrates your commitment to personal and professional growth.
- For instance, you could say, "During my time away, I completed an online certification in project management, which has equipped me with the skills needed for this role."

1. **Reassure Them of Your Readiness:**

- Conclude your explanation by expressing your enthusiasm for re-

entering the workforce and your readiness to contribute. A positive and forward-looking attitude can help alleviate any lingering concerns.
- You might add, "I am excited about the opportunity to bring my skills back into the workforce and contribute positively to your team."

Practice Your Delivery

Before the interview, practice your explanation until it feels natural. Rehearse with a friend or mentor to ensure you convey confidence and authenticity. The more comfortable you are with your narrative, the more convincing it will sound to your interviewer.

Addressing Weaknesses

When asked about weaknesses, interviewers are not seeking a confession of your deepest flaws; instead, they want to see how self-aware you are and how you handle challenges. Transforming potential negatives into growth opportunities is key to successfully answering this question.

Choosing the Right Weakness

When selecting a weakness to discuss, opt for something that won't directly disqualify you from the role but is still genuine. Here are some guidelines for choosing an appropriate weakness:

1. **Relevance to the Position:**

- Select a weakness that is relevant to the job, but not critical. For example, if you're applying for a role that requires teamwork, you might mention that you initially struggle with delegating tasks but are working to improve.

1. **Avoid Clichés:**

- Steer clear of common responses like "I work too hard" or "I'm a perfectionist." These can come off as insincere. Instead, choose a weakness that reflects a real area for growth.

1. **Focus on Improvement:**

- Frame your weakness as a challenge you are actively addressing. This shows your commitment to personal development and resilience.

Structuring Your Response

When responding to questions about your weaknesses, use the following structure to ensure clarity and impact:

1. **Identify the Weakness:**

- Clearly state your weakness without over-explaining. For example: "I have found that I sometimes struggle with public speaking."

1. **Explain Your Efforts to Improve:**

- Discuss specific actions you are taking to address this weakness. For instance: "To tackle this, I enrolled in a public speaking course and have sought out opportunities to present in smaller team meetings."

1. **Highlight Progress:**

- Emphasize any improvements you've made and how you plan to continue developing. For example: "I've already noticed a significant increase in my confidence, and I look forward to further refining this skill as I progress in my career."

Practice Self-Reflection

Before the interview, take time to reflect on your weaknesses and how they have shaped your professional journey. This self-awareness will allow you to speak authentically and engage more meaningfully with the interviewer.

Handling Salary Questions

Discussing salary can be one of the most uncomfortable aspects of the interview process. However, with the right strategies, you can navigate this topic without underselling yourself or creating unnecessary tension.

Timing is Key

When it comes to salary discussions, timing can significantly influence the conversation. Here are some strategies for approaching the topic effectively:

1. **Wait for the Right Moment:**

- If possible, allow the employer to bring up salary first. This not only shows your interest in the role but also gives you insight into their budget and expectations.

1. **Responding to Direct Questions:**

- If asked about your salary expectations, avoid giving a specific number right away. Instead, you might respond with: "I'd like to learn more about the responsibilities of the role and the team before discussing salary expectations."

Research Salary Ranges

Before the interview, conduct thorough research on salary ranges for similar positions in your industry and location. Websites like Glassdoor, Payscale, and LinkedIn Salary Insights can provide valuable data. Consider these factors:

1. **Location:** Salaries can vary significantly based on geographic location, so ensure your research accounts for this.
2. **Experience Level:** Be sure to compare your experience and qualifications to the average salary range for similar roles.
3. **Company Size and Industry:** Larger companies or those in specific

industries may offer higher salaries, so factor this into your expectations.

Preparing Your Response

When it's time to discuss salary, frame your response to reflect your research and qualifications. Here's a structure you can use:

1. **Provide a Salary Range:**

- After researching, present a salary range based on your findings. You might say, "Based on my research and the responsibilities outlined in the job description, I believe a salary range of $X to $Y would be appropriate."

1. **Justify Your Range:**

- Briefly explain your reasoning behind the range. You could say, "This range reflects my skills, experience, and the value I can bring to the team."

1. **Express Flexibility:**

- Conclude by expressing openness to negotiation. For example: "I am open to discussing this further and would like to find a compensation package that reflects my qualifications and the value I bring to the company."

Practice Confidence in Negotiation

Practicing your salary negotiation skills can boost your confidence. Role-play with a friend or mentor, simulating potential scenarios to help you feel more comfortable discussing your salary during the interview.

CHAPTER 7: ANSWERING TOUGH INTERVIEW QUESTIONS

Successfully answering tough interview questions requires preparation, honesty, and confidence. By effectively addressing employment gaps, framing weaknesses as growth opportunities, and navigating salary discussions, you can present yourself as a strong candidate who is self-aware and ready for the challenges of the job. With practice and the right strategies, you can turn these potentially daunting questions into opportunities to showcase your strengths and suitability for the role, ultimately enhancing your chances of success in the interview process.

Chapter 8: Standing Out in Virtual Interviews

In today's job market, virtual interviews have become the norm rather than the exception. The COVID-19 pandemic accelerated this shift, pushing companies and job seekers alike to adapt to a new way of connecting. While virtual interviews offer convenience, they also come with unique challenges that can make it difficult for candidates to stand out. In this chapter, we will explore the key elements of excelling in virtual interviews, from technical preparations to etiquette and maintaining high energy throughout the conversation.

Technical Preparations

Before you even think about what to say in your interview, ensuring that your technical setup is flawless is paramount. The first impression you make is often visual, and in a virtual setting, this impression can be heavily influenced by your equipment and environment. Here are the key aspects to focus on:

1. Setting Up Your Technology
A. Choosing the Right Device

- **Laptop vs. Desktop:** While both can be effective, a laptop is usually preferable for interviews due to its portability and built-in camera and microphone. Ensure that your device has a reliable operating system and is free from software updates or background processes that could slow it

down during the interview.
- **Camera Quality:** The quality of your webcam can significantly impact how you are perceived. If possible, invest in an external webcam that offers at least 720p resolution. High-definition (1080p) cameras provide an even better image, enhancing your appearance.

B. Audio Quality

- **Microphone Considerations:** Sound quality is crucial in virtual interviews. Built-in microphones often don't capture your voice clearly. Consider using an external microphone or a good pair of headphones with a microphone. This setup not only improves sound quality but also helps reduce background noise.
- **Testing Your Setup:** Before the interview, conduct a test run with a friend or family member to ensure that your audio is clear. Ask for feedback on how you sound and if there are any distracting background noises.

C. Internet Connection

- **Wired vs. Wireless:** Whenever possible, use a wired internet connection. Ethernet connections are more stable and reliable than Wi-Fi, reducing the chances of connection issues during the interview.
- **Bandwidth Check:** Test your internet speed using online tools like Speedtest.net. Ensure you have sufficient bandwidth (ideally, at least 10 Mbps upload and download) to support video streaming without interruptions.

2. Creating the Right Environment
A. Lighting

- **Natural Light:** If possible, position yourself facing a window to take advantage of natural light. This will illuminate your face and create a

more inviting atmosphere. Avoid having bright light sources behind you, as they can create a silhouette effect that makes you hard to see.
- **Artificial Lighting:** If natural light isn't available, use soft, diffused lighting sources. A ring light or adjustable desk lamp can provide even illumination. Aim for a warm light that mimics natural daylight, as harsh lighting can create unflattering shadows.

B. Background

- **Clutter-Free Zone:** Your background should be clean and professional. Remove any distracting items or clutter that could divert attention away from you. Ideally, choose a neutral-colored wall or a well-organized area of your home.
- **Virtual Backgrounds:** If your environment is less than ideal, consider using a virtual background. Many video conferencing tools allow you to select a background image or blur your surroundings. However, ensure that the virtual background doesn't distract from your presence; it should look professional and align with the company's culture.

3. Preparing Your Materials
A. Resume and Notes

- **Accessible Documents:** Have your resume and any notes ready and easily accessible during the interview. This may include key points you want to remember or questions you want to ask the interviewer.
- **Digital Format:** Ensure that any documents you plan to share are in a digital format that can be easily shared through the video conferencing platform (e.g., PDF). Familiarize yourself with the sharing feature to avoid fumbling during the interview.

B. Practice Sessions

- **Mock Interviews:** Conduct mock interviews to familiarize yourself

with the technology and practice answering questions. This will not only improve your comfort level with the virtual format but also help you refine your answers.
- **Feedback Loop:** After your practice sessions, ask for constructive feedback on your technical setup, body language, and responses. Use this feedback to make necessary adjustments before the actual interview.

Virtual-Specific Etiquette

Once you have ensured that your technical setup is flawless, it's time to focus on virtual-specific etiquette. The dynamics of a virtual interview differ significantly from those of an in-person interview, making it essential to adapt your behavior accordingly.

1. Maintaining Eye Contact
A. Camera Positioning

- **Direct Eye Contact:** One of the biggest challenges in virtual interviews is maintaining eye contact. To create the illusion of eye contact, position your camera at eye level. This means placing your laptop on a stand or using a stack of books to raise it.
- **Looking at the Camera:** While it's tempting to look at the screen to see the interviewer, try to focus your gaze on the camera. This creates a connection with the interviewer and makes them feel engaged.

B. Avoiding Distractions

- **Minimize Multitasking:** Resist the urge to check your phone or other notifications during the interview. This can signal disinterest or a lack of focus.
- **Turn Off Notifications:** Before the interview, silence notifications on your computer and phone. Consider using "Do Not Disturb" mode to minimize distractions.

2. **Engaging with the Interviewer**
   A. **Verbal Engagement**

   - **Active Listening:** Demonstrate active listening by nodding and using verbal affirmations (like "I see" or "That's interesting") to acknowledge what the interviewer is saying. This shows that you are engaged and value their input.
   - **Pause Before Responding:** In a virtual environment, there can be a slight delay in audio transmission. After the interviewer finishes speaking, take a moment to pause before responding. This helps ensure that you don't interrupt them.

   B. **Expressive Body Language**

   - **Use Hand Gestures:** Incorporate appropriate hand gestures to emphasize your points. This can add warmth and personality to your responses, making you more relatable.
   - **Maintain Good Posture:** Sit up straight and lean slightly forward to convey interest and engagement. Slouching or appearing disinterested can create a negative impression.

Keeping the Energy High

One of the most significant challenges of virtual interviews is keeping the energy level high, especially when you're speaking to a screen rather than a person. However, with the right strategies, you can maintain enthusiasm and presence throughout the conversation.

1. **Bringing Your Personality to the Forefront**
   A. **Authenticity**

   - **Be Yourself:** Let your personality shine through in your responses. Authenticity helps build a connection with the interviewer, making you more memorable. Share anecdotes or stories that highlight your

qualifications, but keep them relevant to the discussion.
- **Show Enthusiasm:** Your enthusiasm for the role and company should be evident in your tone and expressions. Smiling and expressing genuine excitement can make a positive impact.

B. Engaging with the Interviewer

- **Ask Questions:** Engage the interviewer by asking thoughtful questions about the role or company. This demonstrates your interest and allows for a more dynamic conversation. Prepare questions in advance that reflect your research.
- **Find Common Ground:** Look for opportunities to establish rapport. If the interviewer mentions a shared interest or experience, acknowledge it and build on that connection.

2. Using Visual Cues
A. Visual Aids

- **Share Your Screen:** If relevant, consider sharing your screen to present your portfolio or demonstrate a project you've worked on. This visual engagement can enhance your presentation and showcase your skills.
- **Utilize Props:** If appropriate, use props or materials related to your field that can visually engage the interviewer. For example, if you're applying for a graphic design role, having examples of your work in the background can serve as a conversation starter.

3. Practicing Mindfulness and Focus
A. Preparation Techniques

- **Deep Breathing:** Before the interview, practice deep breathing exercises to calm any nerves. This will help you stay focused and composed throughout the conversation.
- **Positive Visualization:** Visualize yourself succeeding in the interview.

This mental exercise can boost your confidence and help you approach the interview with a positive mindset.

B. Energy Management

- **Stay Hydrated:** Drink water before the interview to stay refreshed and alert. A hydrated body supports better cognitive function and concentration.
- **Take Breaks When Necessary:** If you have back-to-back interviews, make sure to take short breaks to reset your energy. Stand up, stretch, and take a few deep breaths to recharge.

In a world increasingly dominated by virtual interactions, standing out in virtual interviews is essential for success in your job search. By investing time and effort into your technical setup, mastering virtual etiquette, and keeping your energy high, you can create a memorable impression on your interviewers. Virtual interviews may present unique challenges, but with the right strategies, you can navigate them with confidence, authenticity, and professionalism. Remember, the goal is not just to land the job but to showcase the best version of yourself, making a lasting impact in this digital age of recruitment.

Chapter 9: Asking Insightful Questions

Asking insightful questions during an interview is one of the most critical aspects of the process that can set you apart from other candidates. Not only does it demonstrate your genuine interest in the role and the organization, but it also provides you with valuable information to determine if the position aligns with your career goals and values. This chapter will explore various strategies for formulating insightful questions, focusing on showing you've done your homework, probing the company's challenges, and revealing company culture.

Questions to Show You've Done Your Homework

1. Researching the Company

To ask thoughtful questions, you first need to research the company thoroughly. Utilize various sources, including the company's website, recent news articles, press releases, and employee reviews on platforms like Glassdoor or LinkedIn. By gathering this information, you can formulate questions that reflect your understanding of the company's operations, goals, and market position.

A. Industry Position and Competitors

One effective way to demonstrate your research is by asking about the company's position within its industry and how it compares to its competitors. This not only shows that you understand the market dynamics but also that you're thinking critically about the company's strategy.

Example Questions:

- "I noticed that [Company Name] has recently launched [Product/Service]. How do you see this impacting your position in the market compared to competitors like [Competitor Name]?"
- "Given the recent shifts in [Industry Trend], how is [Company Name] adapting its strategies to maintain a competitive edge?"

B. Recent Achievements and Goals

Highlighting recent company achievements or future goals can also indicate that you've done your homework. It reflects your interest in the company's direction and can lead to a discussion about how you might contribute to these goals.

Example Questions:

- "Congratulations on the recent [Award/Recognition]! What do you think contributed most to this achievement?"
- "I read that [Company Name] is aiming to [Goal]. How do you see the role I'm applying for contributing to this goal?"

2. Understanding the Role's Impact

Framing questions about how the role you're applying for contributes to the company's objectives not only reflects your research but also your eagerness to be a valuable team member.

Example Questions:

- "How does this position support the company's overall mission and strategic goals?"
- "Can you share how this role has evolved over the past few years and its impact on the team's success?"

CHAPTER 9: ASKING INSIGHTFUL QUESTIONS

Probing the Company's Challenges

Understanding the challenges a company faces can provide you with insights into its operations and culture, allowing you to position yourself as a solution. When you inquire about challenges, it also reflects your strategic thinking and willingness to contribute to problem-solving.

1. Identifying Pain Points

When asking about the company's challenges, focus on strategic issues rather than day-to-day operational problems. This shows that you're thinking critically about the organization's long-term success.

A. Current and Future Challenges

It's crucial to ask about both current and future challenges. This will give you a sense of the company's priorities and how you might fit into the larger picture.

Example Questions:

- "What are some of the biggest challenges [Company Name] is currently facing, and how is the team working to address them?"
- "As [Industry] continues to evolve, what challenges do you foresee in the next few years, and how is the company preparing to tackle them?"

2. Positioning Yourself as a Solution

Once you have a clear understanding of the challenges the company faces, you can use your responses to position yourself as a potential solution. This is where your skills and experiences come into play.

A. Tailoring Your Skills to Their Needs

You can use the information gathered from your questions to highlight how your skills and experiences align with the company's needs. This not only showcases your value but also illustrates your proactive approach.

Example Questions:

- "I understand that [Company Name] is focusing on [Challenge]. With my background in [Relevant Experience], how do you see me contributing

to addressing this issue?"
- "How does this team collaborate to solve challenges, and what role would I play in that process?"

Questions That Reveal Company Culture

Company culture is a critical aspect of any job, impacting job satisfaction and performance. Understanding the company culture will help you determine if it's the right fit for you. Asking the right questions can provide insights into team dynamics, management styles, and the overall work environment.

1. Team Dynamics

Understanding how teams interact within the company can help you assess whether the work environment aligns with your collaboration style and values.

A. Collaboration and Communication

Questions that focus on collaboration and communication styles within the team will provide insights into how you might fit into the company culture.

Example Questions:

- "Can you describe the team I would be working with and how they typically collaborate on projects?"
- "What communication tools and practices does the team use to ensure everyone is aligned and informed?"

2. Management Style and Support

Inquiring about management styles and support structures can reveal a lot about the company's culture. Understanding how managers interact with their teams will help you gauge whether you'd thrive in that environment.

A. Leadership Approach

Questions regarding leadership can help you assess whether the management style aligns with your expectations and preferences.

Example Questions:

- "How would you describe your management style, and what can team members expect in terms of support and feedback?"
- "How does the leadership team foster professional growth and development within the organization?"

3. Work-Life Balance and Values

It's essential to understand the company's stance on work-life balance and values, as these elements directly impact employee satisfaction and well-being.

A. Company Values

Questions regarding the company's core values and how they manifest in daily operations can provide a clearer picture of the organizational culture.

Example Questions:

- "What are the core values of [Company Name], and how do they influence the day-to-day operations?"
- "How does [Company Name] support work-life balance for its employees?"

Asking insightful questions during an interview is a powerful way to demonstrate your interest, research, and critical thinking skills. By formulating questions that reflect your understanding of the company, its challenges, and its culture, you position yourself as a strong candidate who is not only prepared but also eager to contribute. Thoughtful inquiries can help you gain valuable insights that enable you to make an informed decision about the role, ensuring that it aligns with your career aspirations and values. In the competitive landscape of job searching, the ability to ask insightful questions is a key strategy that can set you apart and enhance your candidacy.

Chapter 10: Demonstrating Soft Skills

In the modern workplace, technical expertise alone is not enough to secure a job and thrive in it. Employers increasingly recognize the importance of soft skills—interpersonal abilities that enable individuals to interact effectively and harmoniously with others. This chapter will delve into the significance of soft skills in the hiring process and workplace dynamics, emphasizing emotional intelligence, teamwork, and how to convey these skills effectively during interviews.

Why Soft Skills Matter

1. The Shift in Workplace Demands

Historically, technical skills were prioritized in hiring processes, particularly in fields such as engineering, IT, and finance. However, as workplaces become more collaborative and dynamic, soft skills have taken center stage. Employers are now seeking candidates who not only possess the requisite technical expertise but also the ability to communicate effectively, adapt to changing circumstances, and work well in teams.

A. The Impact of Automation and AI

The rise of automation and artificial intelligence (AI) in the workplace has further underscored the need for soft skills. As machines handle more routine tasks, human workers must focus on the skills that machines cannot replicate, such as creativity, problem-solving, and emotional intelligence. Soft skills have become the differentiators that set candidates apart in a competitive job market.

B. Employee Retention and Workplace Culture

Companies are increasingly aware that soft skills contribute to a positive workplace culture, employee engagement, and retention. Employees with strong interpersonal skills tend to foster better relationships with colleagues, leading to improved collaboration and a more supportive work environment. This, in turn, enhances job satisfaction and reduces turnover rates.

2. Key Soft Skills to Develop

Understanding the specific soft skills that employers value can help candidates tailor their preparation for interviews. Some of the most sought-after soft skills include:

- **Communication:** The ability to express ideas clearly and effectively, both verbally and in writing.
- **Teamwork:** The capacity to work collaboratively with others to achieve common goals.
- **Adaptability:** The willingness and ability to adjust to new challenges, changes, and situations.
- **Problem-solving:** The capability to analyze situations, identify issues, and develop effective solutions.
- **Emotional intelligence:** The ability to recognize and manage one's emotions and the emotions of others.

By honing these skills, candidates can position themselves as well-rounded individuals who are prepared to thrive in any work environment.

Showing Emotional Intelligence

Emotional intelligence (EI) is a crucial component of soft skills that involves recognizing, understanding, and managing emotions—both your own and those of others. Demonstrating emotional intelligence during an interview can significantly impact how you're perceived by hiring managers.

1. The Components of Emotional Intelligence

Emotional intelligence comprises several key components:

- **Self-awareness:** Recognizing your own emotions, strengths, weaknesses, and values, and how they affect your behavior.
- **Self-regulation:** The ability to control impulsive feelings and behaviors, manage stress, and adapt to changing circumstances.
- **Empathy:** Understanding and sharing the feelings of others, which fosters meaningful connections and relationships.
- **Social skills:** The ability to build and maintain healthy relationships, communicate effectively, and resolve conflicts.
- **Motivation:** A drive to achieve for the sake of accomplishment, not just external rewards.

By cultivating these components, candidates can showcase their emotional intelligence during interviews.

2. Demonstrating Empathy and Adaptability

Empathy and adaptability are two essential facets of emotional intelligence that candidates can demonstrate during interviews.

A. Active Listening

Active listening is a powerful way to show empathy during an interview. When responding to interviewers, take the time to listen carefully to their questions and comments. This involves not only hearing the words but also understanding the underlying emotions and intentions. Use verbal and non-verbal cues, such as nodding and maintaining eye contact, to convey your engagement.

Example:

When asked about a challenging experience, instead of simply recounting the events, you might say, "I understand that these situations can be very stressful, both for colleagues and for management. In my previous role, I faced a similar challenge, and I found that taking a step back and actively listening to my team helped us come up with effective solutions together."

B. Sharing Personal Experiences

Sharing relevant personal experiences can also demonstrate your empathy and adaptability. When discussing challenges you've faced, highlight how you considered the perspectives of others and adjusted your approach accordingly.

CHAPTER 10: DEMONSTRATING SOFT SKILLS

Example:

"During a team project, we faced a tight deadline. I realized that one of my teammates was struggling with the workload. Instead of pushing forward alone, I approached them to understand their concerns and we collaboratively redistributed tasks. This not only alleviated their stress but also strengthened our teamwork."

Being a Team Player

In today's collaborative work environments, being a team player is a highly valued trait. Employers are looking for candidates who can contribute positively to a team dynamic and work effectively with diverse groups of people. Here are ways to convey your collaborative spirit during an individual interview.

1. Highlighting Team Experiences

One of the most effective ways to demonstrate your teamwork skills is to highlight your past experiences working in teams. When responding to questions about your work history, focus on specific examples that showcase your ability to collaborate, communicate, and contribute to team success.

A. The STAR Method

Using the STAR method (Situation, Task, Action, Result) can help structure your responses and clearly convey your experiences. This method allows you to present your teamwork abilities in a compelling and organized manner.

Example Response Using STAR:

- **Situation:** "In my previous job at XYZ Corp, our team was tasked with launching a new marketing campaign on a tight deadline."
- **Task:** "As the project manager, my role was to coordinate the efforts of the team and ensure everyone was aligned."
- **Action:** "I organized weekly meetings to discuss progress, encouraged open communication, and facilitated brainstorming sessions. When one of our designers faced challenges, I offered my assistance and worked with them to find solutions."

- **Result:** "As a result, we successfully launched the campaign on time, and it exceeded our initial engagement targets by 30%. The collaboration not only boosted our morale but also improved our overall productivity."

2. Communicating Collaborative Values

It's important to communicate your collaborative values during the interview process. Employers want to hear about your approach to teamwork and how you prioritize building relationships with colleagues.

A. Emphasizing Respect and Open Communication

You can convey your collaborative spirit by discussing the importance of respect and open communication within teams. Highlight your commitment to creating a positive team environment where everyone's contributions are valued.

Example Response:

"I believe that effective teamwork is built on mutual respect and open communication. In my previous role, I made it a priority to create an inclusive environment where team members felt comfortable sharing their ideas and feedback. This approach not only enhanced our creativity but also fostered a strong sense of camaraderie within the team."

3. Asking Questions about Team Dynamics

During the interview, consider asking questions about the company's team dynamics. This not only shows your interest in collaboration but also helps you gauge whether the organization's culture aligns with your values.

Example Questions:

- "Can you describe the team structure I would be working within and how team members collaborate on projects?"
- "How does the company foster a collaborative culture, and what role do team members play in decision-making processes?"

CHAPTER 10: DEMONSTRATING SOFT SKILLS

Demonstrating soft skills is crucial in today's competitive job market, where employers seek candidates who can navigate interpersonal dynamics effectively. By showcasing your emotional intelligence, empathy, adaptability, and teamwork abilities, you can set yourself apart from other candidates. Soft skills not only enhance your employability but also contribute to a positive work environment and long-term career success. By focusing on these skills during interviews, you can present yourself as a well-rounded candidate who is ready to thrive in any organization.

Chapter 11: Following Up After the Interview

The interview process does not end when you walk out the door. In fact, one of the most critical phases often occurs afterward: the follow-up. This chapter will explore the importance of following up after an interview, including writing the perfect thank-you note, knowing when and how to follow up, and turning rejections into future opportunities.

Writing the Perfect Thank You Note

1. The Importance of a Thank You Note

A thank-you note is more than just a polite gesture; it's an opportunity to reinforce your candidacy and express your gratitude. Research shows that sending a thank-you note can set you apart from other candidates. It reflects your professionalism and genuine interest in the position. In a competitive job market, a well-crafted thank-you note can be the deciding factor in the hiring process.

A. A Chance to Reiterate Your Fit

The thank-you note allows you to reinforce why you are the right fit for the role. It's a chance to remind the interviewer of your relevant skills and experiences that align with the company's needs.

B. Building Relationships

Sending a thank-you note also helps build rapport with the interviewer. It shows that you value their time and are genuinely interested in the organization. This can lay the groundwork for a positive relationship, whether or not you get the job.

2. Crafting Your Thank You Note

When writing your thank-you note, consider the following elements to ensure it's effective:

A. Start with a Personal Greeting

Begin with a personalized greeting that includes the interviewer's name. If you interviewed with multiple people, consider sending individual notes to each person.

Example:

"Dear [Interviewer's Name],"

B. Express Your Gratitude

Immediately express your appreciation for the opportunity to interview. Be sincere and specific about what you are thankful for.

Example:

"Thank you for taking the time to meet with me yesterday to discuss the [Job Title] position. I truly appreciate the insights you shared about the company's innovative projects."

C. Reinforce Your Interest and Qualifications

In the body of the note, reaffirm your interest in the position and the company. Highlight specific points from the interview that resonated with you and align with your qualifications.

Example:

"I am even more excited about the possibility of joining [Company Name] after learning about your commitment to [specific company value or project discussed in the interview]. I believe my experience in [relevant skill or experience] would allow me to contribute effectively to your team."

D. Keep It Concise and Professional

Your thank-you note should be concise, ideally no longer than a few short paragraphs. Maintain a professional tone throughout.

E. Closing Thoughts

Close with a positive statement, reiterating your interest in the position and your hope for future communication.

Example:
"Thank you once again for the opportunity. I look forward to the possibility of working together and contributing to the exciting projects at [Company Name]."

F. Sign Off
End with a polite sign-off, followed by your name.

Example:
"Best regards,
[Your Name]"

3. Timing and Delivery
Send your thank-you note within 24 hours of your interview. This promptness shows your enthusiasm and professionalism. Choose a delivery method that aligns with the company's culture; for example, a handwritten note can be more personal, while an email may be more appropriate in fast-paced industries.

When and How to Follow Up

1. The Importance of Timing
Following up after an interview is essential, but timing is key. You want to show your interest without coming across as pushy. Understanding the right moment to check in can make a significant difference in how your follow-up is received.

A. The General Rule of Thumb
A good rule of thumb is to wait about one week after the interview before following up. This gives the hiring team sufficient time to review candidates and discuss their options.

B. When to Follow Up Sooner
If the interviewer mentioned a specific timeline for making a decision, it's best to adhere to that timeline. For instance, if they said they would make a decision within a week, wait until that time has passed to follow up.

2. Crafting Your Follow-Up Message
When it's time to follow up, keep your message brief and focused. Here's

CHAPTER 11: FOLLOWING UP AFTER THE INTERVIEW

how to structure it:

A. Begin with a Polite Greeting

Just like your thank-you note, start with a personal greeting.

Example:

"Dear [Interviewer's Name],"

B. Reference the Interview

Mention the interview date and express your continued interest in the position.

Example:

"I hope this message finds you well. I wanted to follow up on our conversation from [Date of Interview] regarding the [Job Title] position."

C. Inquire About the Hiring Process

Politely ask for an update on the hiring process without sounding demanding.

Example:

"I am very excited about the opportunity to join [Company Name] and would love to hear if there have been any updates regarding my application."

D. Express Gratitude Again

Reiterate your appreciation for their time and consideration.

Example:

"Thank you again for considering my application. I appreciate the time you took to interview me and discuss the exciting initiatives at [Company Name]."

E. Close Professionally

Finish with a polite closing and your name.

Example:

"Best regards,

[Your Name]"

3. What to Avoid in Follow-Ups

While following up is important, there are a few common pitfalls to avoid:

A. Being Too Pushy

Avoid sending multiple follow-up messages or expressing frustration about the lack of communication. This can create a negative impression.

B. Neglecting to Personalize Your Message

Each follow-up should be tailored to the specific interview. A generic message can suggest a lack of genuine interest.

C. Ignoring the Company's Communication Style

Pay attention to the company's communication style. If they prefer formal communication, maintain that tone in your follow-up. If they are more casual, adapt your message accordingly.

Turning Rejections into Opportunities

Receiving a rejection after an interview can be disheartening, but it doesn't have to be the end of the road. Many candidates miss out on valuable opportunities to turn a rejection into future possibilities. Here's how to navigate rejection effectively.

1. Requesting Feedback

One of the most valuable actions you can take after a rejection is to request feedback from the interviewer. This shows your commitment to improvement and allows you to gain insights into your performance.

A. How to Ask for Feedback

When reaching out for feedback, keep your message respectful and appreciative. Here's a structure to follow:

Example Message:

"Dear [Interviewer's Name],

I hope this message finds you well. Thank you for considering my application for the [Job Title] position. While I'm disappointed to hear that I wasn't selected, I truly appreciate the opportunity to interview and learn about [Company Name]. If possible, I would be grateful for any feedback you could provide regarding my interview or application. This feedback would be invaluable as I continue my job search. Thank you again for your time and consideration. Best regards,

[Your Name]"

B. Timing for Feedback Requests

Send your feedback request within a few days of receiving the rejection notice. This shows that you are proactive and eager to learn.

2. Keeping Doors Open for the Future

Just because you received a rejection doesn't mean the door is closed permanently. Maintaining a positive relationship with the interviewer can lead to future opportunities.

A. Expressing Continued Interest

In your follow-up after a rejection, express your continued interest in the company. Let them know that you admire their work and would appreciate being considered for future openings.

Example:

"Although I wasn't selected for the [Job Title] position, I want to express my continued interest in [Company Name]. I admire your commitment to [specific company value or initiative], and I would love the chance to contribute to your team in the future."

B. Connecting on LinkedIn

Consider connecting with your interviewer on LinkedIn. This allows you to stay in touch and keep your name in their mind for future opportunities.

C. Staying Informed About the Company

Keep an eye on the company's job postings and major developments. If you see a new opening that aligns with your skills, don't hesitate to apply again.

Following up after an interview is a critical step in the job search process that can significantly impact your chances of success. Writing a thoughtful thank-you note, knowing when and how to follow up, and turning rejections into opportunities are essential skills for job seekers. By mastering these strategies, you can reinforce your candidacy, maintain positive relationships, and keep doors open for future opportunities. Remember, the interview process is not just about securing a job; it's about building connections and continuously improving your approach. With persistence and professionalism, you can navigate the post-interview landscape effectively and position yourself for success.

Chapter 12: Interviewing for Leadership Roles

When interviewing for leadership roles, candidates face a unique set of challenges and expectations that differ significantly from those for entry-level or even mid-level positions. Leadership interviews are not merely about technical skills or past achievements; they focus heavily on strategic thinking, vision, and the ability to inspire and lead teams. This chapter explores the nuances of interviewing for leadership positions, providing insights into what sets these interviews apart, how to demonstrate strategic thinking, and ways to present yourself as a leader.

What Sets Leadership Interviews Apart

1. The Importance of Vision and Strategy

A. A Different Set of Expectations

Leadership roles, whether in management or executive positions, demand a different set of skills and attributes compared to other positions. Interviewers are not only looking for candidates who can perform tasks but also those who can set a vision and guide others towards achieving that vision. Leadership interviews often focus on strategic thinking, decision-making abilities, and the capacity to navigate complex challenges.

B. Focus on Impact and Influence

In leadership interviews, candidates must articulate their ability to influence others and drive organizational change. The interviewer is interested in understanding how you can impact the organization, the teams you will lead, and the stakeholders involved. This requires candidates to share specific examples that showcase their leadership experiences and the tangible results they've achieved.

2. Behavioral and Situational Questions

A. Increased Emphasis on Behavioral Questions

While behavioral questions are common in all interviews, they take on greater significance in leadership interviews. Interviewers will ask questions that require you to reflect on past experiences, showcasing your leadership style and problem-solving skills. Expect questions like:

- "Can you describe a time when you had to lead a team through a challenging project?"
- "How did you handle a conflict between team members?"

B. Situational Questions

Situational questions are designed to assess how you would handle hypothetical scenarios. For leadership positions, these questions often focus on strategic decision-making, team dynamics, and conflict resolution. Examples include:

- "If your team is facing a tight deadline and a key member is underperforming, how would you address the situation?"
- "How would you prioritize competing projects with limited resources?"

3. Emphasizing Cultural Fit and Leadership Style

A. Assessing Fit Within the Organization

For leadership roles, cultural fit is crucial. Interviewers will assess whether your values align with the organization's mission and culture. You may be asked about your leadership philosophy and how it complements the company's vision. Be prepared to discuss:

- Your approach to team collaboration.
- Your views on employee engagement and motivation.
- How you navigate organizational politics.

B. Leadership Style and Philosophy

Interviewers will also be interested in understanding your leadership style. Are you a collaborative leader who values team input, or are you more directive in your approach? Be prepared to articulate your leadership philosophy and provide examples of how it has shaped your interactions with team members.

4. Assessing Soft Skills and Emotional Intelligence

A. The Role of Soft Skills in Leadership

In leadership roles, soft skills are just as important as technical competencies. Interviewers will evaluate your emotional intelligence, communication skills, and ability to build relationships. You might encounter questions like:

- "How do you approach giving feedback to team members?"
- "Can you share an example of how you've navigated a challenging interpersonal situation?"

B. Building Trust and Credibility

Leaders need to inspire trust and credibility among their teams. Be prepared to discuss how you establish rapport, foster open communication, and create a safe environment for team members to express their ideas and concerns.

Demonstrating Strategic Thinking

1. Framing Your Answers for Long-Term Vision

A. Showcasing a Strategic Mindset

When responding to interview questions, it's essential to frame your answers in a way that reflects your strategic thinking. Use the following strategies to demonstrate your long-term vision:

- **Highlight Big-Picture Thinking**: Discuss your ability to analyze market trends and anticipate changes in the industry. Share examples of how you have adapted strategies based on these insights.
- **Connect Actions to Outcomes**: When discussing past experiences, connect your actions to the larger goals of the organization. For instance, if you implemented a new process, explain how it aligned with the company's strategic objectives.

B. Incorporating Data and Metrics

In leadership roles, decisions are often data-driven. When discussing your past accomplishments, incorporate data and metrics to illustrate your impact. This demonstrates your analytical skills and ability to leverage information for strategic decision-making.

Example: "At [Previous Company], I led a team that streamlined our supply chain processes, resulting in a 15% reduction in costs over two years. This was crucial in positioning the company to compete more effectively in the market."

2. Articulating Your Decision-Making Process

A. The Importance of a Thoughtful Approach

Leadership often involves making difficult decisions. Interviewers will want to understand your decision-making process. Be prepared to discuss:

- **How You Gather Information**: Describe the methods you use to gather relevant information before making a decision. This could include data analysis, team input, or market research.
- **Evaluating Risks and Benefits**: Discuss how you assess potential risks and benefits associated with various options. This showcases your ability to think critically and strategically.

B. Using the STAR Method for Strategic Questions

The STAR (Situation, Task, Action, Result) method can be especially effective when answering questions about strategic decision-making. Here's how to structure your responses:

- **Situation**: Set the context by describing the scenario you faced.
- **Task**: Explain the specific challenge or decision you needed to address.
- **Action**: Detail the steps you took to analyze the situation and arrive at a decision.
- **Result**: Share the outcome of your decision, emphasizing the positive impact on the organization.

Example: "In my previous role, we faced declining sales in a key product line (Situation). My task was to evaluate potential changes to our marketing strategy (Task). I conducted market research and analyzed customer feedback, ultimately recommending a rebranding campaign (Action). As a result, we saw a 30% increase in sales over the next quarter (Result)."

Presenting Yourself as a Leader

1. Building Your Personal Brand

A. Defining Your Leadership Identity

To present yourself as a leader, it's essential to have a clear understanding of your leadership identity. Consider the following:

- **Core Values**: What values drive your leadership style? This could include integrity, collaboration, innovation, or accountability.
- **Unique Strengths**: Identify the strengths that set you apart as a leader. This could be your ability to inspire teams, your strategic vision, or your expertise in a particular area.

B. Communicating Your Brand

When interviewing for leadership positions, be intentional about communicating your personal brand. Use your responses to showcase your values and strengths consistently. For instance, if collaboration is a core value, highlight experiences where you fostered teamwork and inclusivity.

C. Online Presence and Networking

In today's digital age, your online presence is crucial for building your personal brand. Ensure that your LinkedIn profile and other professional social media accounts reflect your leadership identity. Engage in networking opportunities to connect with industry leaders and peers.

2. Demonstrating Leadership Through Actions

A. Sharing Leadership Experiences

When discussing your qualifications, share specific experiences that highlight your leadership abilities. Use the STAR method to frame your stories effectively. Focus on instances where you:

- **Led Teams**: Share experiences where you took charge of a project or initiative, emphasizing your role in guiding and motivating others.
- **Managed Change**: Discuss your experiences in leading teams through change, highlighting how you navigated challenges and supported your team members.

Example: "At [Previous Company], I led a team through a significant organizational restructuring. I focused on transparent communication and provided support to team members, resulting in a smooth transition and high employee morale."

3. Cultivating Executive Presence

A. The Importance of Executive Presence

Executive presence refers to the qualities that make someone a credible and effective leader. This includes confidence, gravitas, and the ability to communicate effectively. Cultivating executive presence can enhance your chances of success in leadership interviews.

B. Non-Verbal Communication

Non-verbal cues play a significant role in how others perceive your leadership capabilities. Pay attention to your body language, eye contact, and posture during the interview. Aim to:

- **Exude Confidence**: Maintain an upright posture, make eye contact, and use hand gestures appropriately to convey confidence.
- **Be Engaging**: Show enthusiasm and engagement in the conversation. This helps establish a connection with the interviewer.

4. Preparing for Leadership Assessments

A. The Growing Trend of Leadership Assessments

Some organizations may require candidates for leadership roles to undergo assessments or evaluations. These may include personality tests, leadership simulations, or case studies. Be prepared for this possibility.

B. Understanding Your Leadership Style

Before any assessment, take time to reflect on your leadership style and approach. Familiarize yourself with common leadership assessments, such as the Myers-Briggs Type Indicator (MBTI) or the DiSC assessment, and understand how they may apply to your leadership identity.

CHAPTER 12: INTERVIEWING FOR LEADERSHIP ROLES

Interviewing for leadership roles requires a distinct approach that emphasizes strategic thinking, personal branding, and the ability to inspire and lead others. By understanding what sets leadership interviews apart, demonstrating strategic thinking, and presenting yourself as a credible leader, you can position yourself for success in this competitive landscape. Embrace the challenges that come with leadership interviews, and use the insights and strategies outlined in this chapter to make a lasting impression. Your journey toward securing a leadership position begins long before the interview itself; it's about building a strong foundation of leadership experiences, cultivating your personal brand, and continuously developing your strategic mindset.

Chapter 13: Handling Group and Panel Interviews

Group and panel interviews present unique challenges for candidates, requiring a blend of interpersonal skills, strategic communication, and adaptability. Unlike traditional one-on-one interviews, these formats involve multiple interviewers or candidates, creating a dynamic environment that can be both intimidating and exhilarating. This chapter will delve into the intricacies of managing group and panel interviews, providing strategies for keeping calm, engaging effectively, balancing attention among panel members, and excelling in collaborative exercises.

Managing Multiple Interviewers

1. Understanding the Format

A. Different Types of Group Interviews

Group interviews can vary in format, but they typically fall into one of two categories:

- **Panel Interviews**: In these interviews, a candidate meets with several interviewers at once, each representing different departments or levels within the organization. The panelists may ask questions alternately or engage in a more conversational format.

- **Group Interviews**: In this setting, multiple candidates interview simultaneously, often through discussions or activities. Interviewers observe interactions among candidates to assess how well they collaborate and communicate.

B. Anticipating Dynamics

Understanding the dynamics at play in group interviews is crucial for managing the experience effectively. Panel interviews may feel more formal, while group interviews can foster a competitive atmosphere. Regardless of the format, candidates should expect to engage with various personalities, which requires adaptability and social awareness.

2. Keeping Calm Under Pressure

A. Preparation is Key

Preparation is essential for handling the nerves that come with group and panel interviews. Here are some tips:

- **Research the Interviewers**: Familiarize yourself with the backgrounds and roles of each panel member. Knowing who you're speaking with can help you feel more comfortable and guide your responses.
- **Practice Responses**: Anticipate questions you might encounter and practice your responses. Rehearsing will enhance your confidence and help you articulate your thoughts clearly.
- **Simulate the Environment**: Consider conducting mock interviews with friends or colleagues, simulating a group or panel format. This will help you get accustomed to speaking in front of multiple people and receiving varied feedback.

B. Mindfulness Techniques

To manage anxiety during the interview, consider employing mindfulness techniques:

- **Deep Breathing**: Practice deep breathing exercises before and during the interview to calm your nerves and center yourself. Take a few slow, deep breaths to relax your body and mind.
- **Positive Visualization**: Visualize a successful interview experience, imagining yourself engaging confidently with the panel and answering questions effectively. This mental rehearsal can help alleviate anxiety.

3. Engaging a Group Effectively

A. Establishing Presence

When faced with multiple interviewers, establishing a strong presence is crucial. Here's how to do it:

- **Make Eye Contact**: Aim to make eye contact with each panel member as you speak. This creates a connection and shows that you value their presence and input.
- **Use Body Language**: Employ confident body language by sitting up straight, smiling, and using gestures to emphasize your points. A confident posture can help convey your competence.

B. Active Listening

Demonstrating active listening is vital for engaging the group effectively. Consider the following strategies:

- **Nod and Acknowledge**: Show that you are listening by nodding or using verbal affirmations like "I see" or "That makes sense." This encourages a positive interaction and indicates your attentiveness.
- **Paraphrase Questions**: When responding to a question, paraphrase it to show that you've understood the inquiry. For example, "That's an interesting question about my experience with team collaboration…" This can also give you a moment to collect your thoughts.

4. Answering Questions Strategically

A. Addressing Multiple Interviewers

In a panel interview, each interviewer may have different styles and questions. Here are tips for addressing them effectively:

- **Direct Responses**: When answering a question, direct your response to the interviewer who posed it initially. After addressing them, make eye contact with the other panel members to engage them as well.
- **Tailor Your Responses**: Consider the specific interests or roles of each interviewer when answering. For instance, if a technical lead asks about your programming skills, focus on relevant experiences that resonate with their expertise.

B. Maintaining Control of the Conversation

In group interviews, it's easy for discussions to veer off course. Here's how to maintain control:

- **Stay Focused**: When you're asked a question, stay focused on that question and avoid straying into unrelated topics. If discussions begin to wander, gently steer the conversation back by reiterating key points.
- **Encourage Collaboration**: If a group interview involves discussions among candidates, encourage collaboration rather than competition. For instance, you can say, "I think we all have valuable insights; let's combine our ideas to tackle this challenge."

Balancing Attention Between Panel Members

1. Building Rapport with Each Interviewer

A. Understanding Each Interviewer's Role

To build rapport effectively, it's essential to understand the unique perspectives each panel member brings to the interview. Here are some considerations:

- **Identify Key Roles**: Determine the roles of each interviewer (e.g., HR, department head, team lead) and tailor your approach accordingly. HR may focus on cultural fit, while a department head may be more interested in technical skills.
- **Show Genuine Interest**: When engaging with each panel member, express genuine interest in their perspectives. Ask questions that reflect their expertise or experiences within the organization.

B. Engaging Individual Interviewers

During the interview, make a conscious effort to engage each panel member. Here's how:

- **Address Each Member**: As you answer questions, make a point to address each member of the panel. For example, after responding to one interviewer, you could turn to another and ask for their thoughts or feedback.
- **Incorporate Names**: Use the names of the interviewers in your responses when appropriate. This adds a personal touch and demonstrates that you value their input.

2. Reading the Room

A. Observing Non-Verbal Cues

Pay attention to the non-verbal cues of each interviewer. Understanding their reactions can help you gauge their level of interest and adjust your approach accordingly:

- **Facial Expressions**: Observe facial expressions to assess engagement. Nods or smiles indicate interest, while furrowed brows may suggest confusion or disinterest.
- **Body Language**: Notice how interviewers lean in or cross their arms.

Leaning in typically signifies engagement, while crossed arms may indicate defensiveness or skepticism.

B. Adjusting Your Delivery

Based on the feedback you receive from the panel, be prepared to adjust your delivery:

- **Changing Tone or Pace**: If you notice that some interviewers seem disengaged, consider varying your tone or pace to capture their attention.
- **Redirecting Attention**: If one panel member is particularly quiet, you might direct a question toward them or ask for their opinion to encourage participation.

Handling Group Exercises

1. Understanding Group Exercises

A. Types of Group Exercises

Group exercises can take various forms, including:

- **Case Studies**: Participants work together to analyze a business problem and present solutions.
- **Role-Playing Scenarios**: Candidates may engage in role-playing exercises that simulate workplace situations.
- **Collaborative Tasks**: These tasks require candidates to work together to accomplish a goal, such as solving a puzzle or planning a project.

B. Importance of Collaboration

Group exercises are designed to assess not only your individual skills but also your ability to collaborate and communicate effectively with others. Interviewers will observe how you interact, contribute, and lead in group settings.

2. Strategies for Excelling in Collaborative Tasks

A. Establishing Your Role

When participating in group exercises, consider establishing a clear role early on. This doesn't mean dominating the conversation; rather, it involves positioning yourself as a contributor. Here are some strategies:

- **Assess Group Dynamics**: Observe the dynamics of the group to identify where you can add value. If someone is leading the discussion, consider how you can support their efforts.
- **Offer Ideas**: Share your thoughts and ideas, but also encourage others to contribute. Use phrases like, "I think we should consider…" followed by, "What do you all think?" This shows you value collaboration.

B. Balancing Contributions

While it's essential to contribute to discussions, be mindful of balancing your input with the contributions of others:

- **Avoid Dominating the Conversation**: Ensure that you're not monopolizing the conversation. Allow others to speak and actively listen to their ideas.
- **Encourage Participation**: If you notice quieter group members, invite them to share their thoughts. You might say, "I'd love to hear your perspective on this, [Name]."

3. Demonstrating Leadership in Group Settings

A. Facilitating Discussion

Even if you're not in a designated leadership role, you can demonstrate leadership qualities by facilitating discussions:

- **Guide Conversations**: Help steer the discussion by summarizing key points and asking follow-up questions. This shows that you're engaged

and invested in the group's success.
- **Encourage Diverse Opinions**: Foster an inclusive environment by encouraging diverse perspectives. You could say, "It's important that we hear from everyone; let's go around the table and share our thoughts."

B. Problem-Solving Skills

Group exercises often involve problem-solving. Showcase your problem-solving skills by:

- **Identifying Challenges**: If the group encounters obstacles, help identify the challenges and propose potential solutions.
- **Collaborating on Solutions**: Work collaboratively to brainstorm and refine solutions. This highlights your ability to work effectively within a team.

Handling group and panel interviews requires a unique set of skills, from managing multiple interviewers to engaging in collaborative exercises. By preparing adequately, building rapport, and demonstrating effective communication, candidates can navigate these challenging interview formats with confidence. Embrace the opportunity to showcase your strengths, connect with interviewers, and shine in the dynamic environment of group and panel interviews. Through practice and strategic thinking, you can transform these challenging scenarios into opportunities for professional growth and success.

Chapter 14: Overcoming Nerves and Anxiety

Feeling nervous before an interview is a common experience for many candidates, regardless of their level of expertise or experience. The pressure to perform, coupled with the uncertainty of the outcome, can trigger anxiety and self-doubt. However, with the right strategies, you can learn to manage these feelings, build your confidence, and present your best self during interviews. This chapter will explore mental preparation techniques, the power of visualization, and strategies for dealing with imposter syndrome.

Mental Preparation Techniques

Mental preparation is essential for minimizing nerves and anxiety before an interview. Various techniques can help you feel more in control and focused, enabling you to present yourself confidently.

1. Breathing Exercises

One of the simplest yet most effective ways to calm nerves is through controlled breathing. Deep breathing techniques can help slow your heart rate, reduce feelings of anxiety, and ground you in the present moment.

A. Diaphragmatic Breathing

Diaphragmatic breathing, or abdominal breathing, encourages full oxygen exchange and promotes relaxation. Here's how to practice it:

- **Find a Comfortable Position**: Sit or lie down in a comfortable position where you can relax.
- **Place Your Hand on Your Belly**: This will help you feel your diaphragm move as you breathe.
- **Inhale Deeply**: Take a deep breath in through your nose, allowing your abdomen to rise as you fill your lungs with air.
- **Exhale Slowly**: Release the breath through your mouth, feeling your abdomen lower. Aim for a longer exhale than inhale.
- **Repeat**: Continue this process for several minutes, focusing on your breath and letting go of any tension in your body.

B. 4-7-8 Breathing Technique

The 4-7-8 breathing technique is another effective method for calming nerves:

- **Inhale for 4 Seconds**: Breathe in deeply through your nose for a count of four.
- **Hold for 7 Seconds**: Hold your breath for a count of seven.
- **Exhale for 8 Seconds**: Slowly breathe out through your mouth for a count of eight.
- **Repeat**: Perform this cycle four times, focusing on the rhythm of your breath and allowing your body to relax.

2. Progressive Muscle Relaxation

Progressive muscle relaxation (PMR) involves systematically tensing and relaxing different muscle groups in your body to alleviate physical tension and anxiety.

A. How to Practice PMR

- **Start from Your Feet**: Begin with your toes, tensing the muscles for a

count of five, then relaxing them completely.
- **Work Your Way Up**: Move to your calves, thighs, abdomen, chest, arms, shoulders, neck, and face. For each muscle group, tense for five seconds and then release.
- **Focus on Sensations**: As you relax each muscle group, focus on the sensations of relaxation and let go of any tension.
- **End with Deep Breathing**: Conclude your PMR session with deep breathing to further enhance relaxation.

3. Mindfulness Meditation

Mindfulness meditation helps you stay present and reduces anxiety by focusing your mind on the current moment. Here's a simple mindfulness practice to try before your interview:

A. Simple Mindfulness Exercise

- **Find a Quiet Space**: Choose a quiet place where you won't be disturbed.
- **Sit Comfortably**: Sit in a comfortable position with your back straight.
- **Focus on Your Breath**: Close your eyes and focus on your breath. Notice the sensation of the air entering and leaving your body.
- **Acknowledge Thoughts**: If thoughts arise, acknowledge them without judgment and gently return your focus to your breath.
- **Practice for a Few Minutes**: Aim to practice mindfulness for five to ten minutes, gradually increasing the duration as you become more comfortable.

The Power of Visualization

Visualization is a powerful technique that involves creating a mental image of a successful outcome. By envisioning yourself succeeding in the interview, you can enhance your confidence and reduce anxiety.

CHAPTER 14: OVERCOMING NERVES AND ANXIETY

1. Understanding Visualization

Visualization works by stimulating the same brain areas that are activated during real-life experiences. When you visualize success, you create a mental blueprint for your performance, helping you prepare for the actual event.

2. How to Practice Visualization

A. Create a Quiet Space

- **Find a Comfortable Position**: Sit or lie down in a comfortable position in a quiet space.
- **Close Your Eyes**: Close your eyes and take a few deep breaths to relax.

B. Envision Your Success

- **Imagine the Scenario**: Picture yourself walking into the interview room with confidence. Imagine the environment, the people, and the atmosphere.
- **Visualize Positive Interactions**: See yourself engaging positively with the interviewers. Imagine answering questions confidently and articulately.
- **Focus on Your Feelings**: Pay attention to how you feel during this visualization. Feel the confidence, excitement, and satisfaction of performing well.

C. Reinforce Your Visualization

- **Repeat the Process**: Practice this visualization exercise regularly, ideally in the days leading up to the interview.
- **Combine with Affirmations**: Pair your visualization with positive affirmations, such as "I am confident and capable" or "I will succeed in this interview."

3. Benefits of Visualization

A. Increased Confidence
Visualization can significantly enhance your self-confidence by mentally preparing you for the interview. When you envision yourself succeeding, you create a sense of familiarity and ease.

B. Reduced Anxiety
By visualizing success, you can alleviate anxiety associated with the unknown. This mental preparation can help you feel more in control and relaxed during the actual interview.

Dealing with Imposter Syndrome

Imposter syndrome is a psychological pattern where individuals doubt their accomplishments and fear being exposed as a "fraud." Many candidates experience these feelings, especially in high-stakes situations like interviews.

1. Understanding Imposter Syndrome

A. Recognizing the Symptoms
Imposter syndrome can manifest in various ways, including:

- **Self-Doubt**: Feeling unworthy of your achievements and questioning your skills.
- **Fear of Exposure**: Worrying that others will discover you're not as competent as they perceive you to be.
- **Attributing Success to Luck**: Dismissing your accomplishments as mere luck rather than the result of your hard work and talent.

B. Common Triggers
Imposter syndrome is often triggered by new challenges or high expectations. Interviews can exacerbate these feelings as candidates compare themselves to perceived standards.

2. Strategies to Manage Imposter Syndrome

A. Acknowledge Your Feelings

Recognizing that you're experiencing imposter syndrome is the first step in overcoming it. Acknowledge your feelings without judgment and remind yourself that many others share similar experiences.

B. Reframe Negative Thoughts

Challenge negative thoughts associated with imposter syndrome by reframing them into positive affirmations. For example:

- **Negative Thought**: "I'm not qualified for this role."
- **Reframed Thought**: "I have valuable skills and experiences that make me a strong candidate."

C. Celebrate Your Achievements

Take time to reflect on and celebrate your accomplishments. Keep a list of your achievements, positive feedback, and successful projects to remind yourself of your capabilities.

D. Seek Support

Reach out to mentors, friends, or colleagues who can provide support and encouragement. Discussing your feelings with others can help you gain perspective and reduce feelings of isolation.

3. Embracing Your Unique Value

A. Identify Your Strengths

Focus on identifying and embracing your unique strengths and contributions. Consider what sets you apart from other candidates and how your experiences make you a valuable asset.

B. Adopt a Growth Mindset

Embrace a growth mindset by viewing challenges as opportunities for learning and growth. Understand that making mistakes is part of the process and can lead to valuable insights.

Overcoming nerves and anxiety before an interview is achievable with the right mental preparation techniques and strategies. By practicing breathing exercises, progressive muscle relaxation, mindfulness, and visualization, you can calm your nerves and build your confidence. Additionally, addressing imposter syndrome is essential for managing self-doubt and embracing your unique strengths.

As you prepare for your next interview, remember that feeling nervous is a normal part of the process. By employing these techniques and strategies, you can transform your anxiety into a source of motivation, enabling you to present your best self and shine in any interview setting.

Chapter 15: Leveraging Your Network for Success

In the ever-evolving landscape of job hunting and career advancement, leveraging your professional network has become more crucial than ever. Networking is not just about collecting business cards or adding connections on LinkedIn; it's about building and nurturing meaningful relationships that can lead to new opportunities, referrals, and invaluable insights. This chapter delves into the power of professional connections, strategies for maintaining relationships post-interview, and the significance of insider information when seeking job opportunities.

Using Professional Connections

1. Understanding the Importance of Networking

Networking can significantly enhance your career prospects. Studies have shown that a significant percentage of jobs are filled through referrals and networking rather than traditional job applications. Here are a few reasons why networking is so vital:

- **Access to Hidden Job Markets**: Many job openings are never publicly advertised. Networking allows you to tap into these hidden opportunities.
- **Credibility Through Recommendations**: A referral from someone

inside the company can carry more weight than a resume submitted through a job board.
- **Building Industry Knowledge**: Engaging with your network can provide insights into industry trends, best practices, and the skills needed to thrive.

2. Identifying Your Network

Before you can leverage your network, you need to identify who is in it. Your network may include:

- **Colleagues and Former Coworkers**: People you've worked with in the past can provide valuable referrals and insights.
- **Alumni**: Fellow graduates from your school can be a great resource, as alumni networks often provide access to job boards and mentorship opportunities.
- **Industry Professionals**: Attend industry events and conferences to meet professionals in your field. Building relationships at these events can lead to valuable connections.
- **Social Media Contacts**: Platforms like LinkedIn are essential for connecting with industry professionals and staying informed about job opportunities.

3. Effectively Leveraging Contacts for Referrals and Recommendations

Once you've identified your network, the next step is to leverage those connections effectively. Here's how:

A. Reach Out with Purpose

- **Personalize Your Message**: When contacting someone for a referral or recommendation, personalize your message. Mention how you know each other and why you're reaching out.

- **Be Clear About Your Request**: Clearly articulate what you're asking for. Whether it's a referral, advice, or insight, being specific helps the other person understand how they can help.

B. Build Your Value Proposition

- **Highlight Your Strengths**: When requesting a referral, remind the person of your skills and accomplishments. This helps them feel confident in recommending you.
- **Share Your Career Goals**: Let your connections know what type of roles you're seeking. This will make it easier for them to refer you to relevant opportunities.

C. Express Gratitude

- **Thank Your Contacts**: Always express gratitude for any help or advice you receive. A simple thank-you note or message can go a long way in strengthening your relationship.
- **Offer Help in Return**: Networking is a two-way street. Look for opportunities to assist your connections in their career endeavors.

4. Best Practices for Networking

A. Attend Networking Events

- **Engage in Industry Conferences**: Attend conferences, workshops, and seminars in your field. These events provide excellent opportunities to meet potential contacts.
- **Join Professional Associations**: Becoming a member of relevant associations allows you to connect with industry professionals and access exclusive job postings.

B. Utilize Social Media

- **Optimize Your LinkedIn Profile**: Ensure your LinkedIn profile is up to date and reflects your professional accomplishments. Engage with your network by sharing relevant content and commenting on posts.
- **Participate in Online Communities**: Join online forums, groups, or discussions related to your industry. Engaging with others can lead to meaningful connections.

C. Schedule Informational Interviews

- **Request Informational Interviews**: Reach out to professionals in your network and request informational interviews to learn more about their careers and the industry.
- **Prepare Thoughtful Questions**: When conducting informational interviews, prepare questions that demonstrate your genuine interest in their experiences and insights.

Building Relationships After the Interview

1. The Importance of Post-Interview Networking

The interview process doesn't end once you leave the interview room. Following up and maintaining relationships with your interviewers can significantly impact your chances of securing the position and advancing your career. Here are some strategies to consider:

2. Following Up After the Interview

A. Crafting a Thoughtful Thank-You Note

- **Send a Personalized Message**: After the interview, send a personalized thank-you note or email to each interviewer. Mention specific points discussed during the interview to reinforce your interest.
- **Express Gratitude**: Thank them for the opportunity to interview and for

their time. This simple gesture shows professionalism and appreciation.

B. Restate Your Interest

- **Reiterate Your Enthusiasm**: In your thank-you note, express your excitement about the role and the company. Highlight how your skills align with the position.
- **Address Any Concerns**: If any concerns arose during the interview, use the thank-you note as an opportunity to address them positively.

3. Maintaining Contact with Interviewers

A. Connect on LinkedIn

- **Send Connection Requests**: After the interview, send LinkedIn connection requests to your interviewers. Include a personalized message mentioning your interview and expressing your desire to stay connected.
- **Engage with Their Content**: Once connected, engage with their posts by liking, commenting, or sharing relevant content. This keeps you on their radar and demonstrates your continued interest.

B. Follow Up Periodically

- **Check In Regularly**: Periodically reach out to your interviewers, especially if you learn something relevant to the conversation you had. This could be sharing an article or a piece of news related to the company.
- **Offer Updates**: If you receive an offer or take on a new position, consider sharing your achievements with them. This reinforces your professional relationship.

4. Building Relationships with Colleagues and Peers

Networking isn't solely about connecting with high-level professionals; your peers and colleagues can be valuable allies in your career journey.

A. Collaborate on Projects

- **Engage in Collaborative Efforts**: If you work with colleagues, seek opportunities to collaborate on projects or initiatives. This builds rapport and strengthens relationships.
- **Offer Support**: Be proactive in offering help or support to your colleagues. Building a reputation as a reliable team member can enhance your network.

B. Join Professional Development Groups

- **Participate in Workshops or Training**: Join groups focused on professional development within your industry. These gatherings can help you connect with like-minded individuals.
- **Engage in Discussion Forums**: Participate in discussion forums or groups related to your field. Sharing insights and learning from others can expand your network.

Getting Insider Information

1. The Value of Insider Information

When applying for jobs, having insider information can give you a significant edge. Knowing about the company culture, team dynamics, and even the challenges the organization is facing can help you tailor your approach and answers during interviews.

2. Strategies for Gaining Insider Information

A. Leverage Your Network

- **Ask Current Employees**: Reach out to current or former employees of the company to gather insights. They can provide valuable information about the work environment, management style, and potential challenges.
- **Utilize Alumni Connections**: If you share an alma mater with someone at the company, reach out for insights. Alumni are often willing to help fellow graduates.

B. Attend Industry Events

- **Network at Conferences**: Attend industry conferences where employees from your target company might be present. Engage in conversations and ask about their experiences with the company.
- **Join Webinars or Panels**: Participate in webinars or panels featuring company representatives. These events can provide insights into the company's values and initiatives.

3. Researching Company Culture

A. Utilize Online Resources

- **Check Company Websites**: Explore the company's website for information about its values, mission, and culture. Look for employee testimonials and case studies.
- **Read Reviews on Job Sites**: Websites like Glassdoor provide insights into employee experiences, company culture, and management practices.

B. Engage with Employees on Social Media

- **Follow the Company on LinkedIn**: Engage with the company's posts

and articles on LinkedIn. This can lead to conversations with employees and provide insights into their culture.
- **Join Relevant Groups**: Join LinkedIn groups or forums related to the company's industry. Engaging in discussions can help you gather valuable insights.

4. Asking Insightful Questions

During the interview process, asking insightful questions can help you gain deeper insights into the company and its culture.

A. Inquire About Company Values

- **Ask About Company Culture**: Questions like "How would you describe the company culture?" or "What qualities do successful employees possess?" can reveal valuable insights.
- **Probing for Challenges**: Inquire about current challenges the team or company is facing. This demonstrates your interest and helps you position yourself as a potential solution.

B. Understand Team Dynamics

- **Ask About Team Collaboration**: Questions like "How does the team collaborate on projects?" can provide insights into the work environment.
- **Inquire About Leadership Style**: Asking about the leadership style of the team can help you understand how decisions are made and how employees are supported.

Leveraging your network for success is a powerful strategy in today's competitive job market. By effectively utilizing your professional connections, building relationships after interviews, and seeking insider information, you can enhance your career prospects and navigate the job search process with confidence.

Networking is not merely a transactional endeavor; it's about cultivating genuine relationships that benefit both you and your connections. As you build and nurture your professional network, remember that every interaction is an opportunity to learn, grow, and pave the way for future success. Your network is your net worth, and by investing in these relationships, you are setting yourself up for long-term career advancement and fulfillment.

Chapter 16: Preparing for Behavioral Assessments

As job seekers increasingly find themselves navigating a competitive landscape, employers are refining their selection processes to ensure they identify the best candidates for their organizations. One key element of this evolution is the integration of behavioral assessments. These assessments go beyond traditional interviews and resumes, providing deeper insights into candidates' psychological traits, problem-solving abilities, and emotional intelligence. This chapter aims to equip you with the knowledge and strategies needed to excel in behavioral assessments, ensuring you stand out from the competition.

Understanding Psychometric Tests

1. What Are Psychometric Tests?

Psychometric tests are standardized assessments designed to measure an individual's mental capabilities, personality traits, and behavioral style. These tests are widely used in various industries and serve as a valuable tool for employers to evaluate candidates' suitability for specific roles.

Types of Psychometric Tests

- **Cognitive Ability Tests**: Assess logical reasoning, numerical ability, verbal comprehension, and spatial awareness. These tests gauge your

problem-solving skills and intellectual capacity.
- **Personality Tests**: Measure your personality traits, preferences, and behavioral tendencies. These assessments often explore dimensions such as openness, conscientiousness, extraversion, agreeableness, and emotional stability.
- **Emotional Intelligence (EI) Tests**: Evaluate your ability to recognize and manage emotions in yourself and others. These tests focus on interpersonal skills, empathy, and emotional regulation.
- **Situational Judgment Tests (SJTs)**: Present hypothetical scenarios related to the workplace and assess how you would respond to them. SJTs help employers gauge your decision-making and problem-solving abilities.

2. Why Employers Use Psychometric Tests

Employers use psychometric tests for several reasons:

- **Objective Evaluation**: These tests provide an objective measure of a candidate's abilities and traits, minimizing the subjectivity of traditional interviews.
- **Predicting Job Performance**: Research has shown that certain personality traits and cognitive abilities correlate with job performance, making these assessments valuable for predicting success in specific roles.
- **Cultural Fit**: Employers want to ensure that candidates align with their organizational culture. Personality tests can help assess whether your values and behaviors fit the company's ethos.

3. Preparing for Psychometric Tests

Preparation is key to performing well in psychometric tests. Here are some effective strategies:

A. Familiarize Yourself with Common Tests

- **Research Common Assessments**: Familiarize yourself with commonly used psychometric tests in your industry. Resources like practice tests and sample questions can help you understand what to expect.
- **Identify the Purpose**: Understand the specific competencies being assessed in each test. This will help you tailor your preparation.

B. Practice Cognitive Ability Tests

- **Take Practice Tests**: There are numerous online platforms that offer practice tests for cognitive ability assessments. Regular practice can help you improve your skills and speed.
- **Focus on Weak Areas**: Identify areas where you struggle and concentrate on improving those specific skills. This targeted approach can enhance your overall performance.

C. Reflect on Personality Traits

- **Self-Assessment**: Before taking personality tests, reflect on your traits and behaviors. Consider how you align with the qualities commonly valued in your target role.
- **Practice Honesty**: While it's natural to want to present yourself positively, aim for honesty in your responses. Most personality tests are designed to detect inconsistencies and inauthentic answers.

4. What to Expect During the Assessment

Psychometric tests can vary in format, but they generally include multiple-choice questions, situational scenarios, or open-ended responses. Here are some things to expect:

- **Time Constraints**: Many tests are timed, so manage your time wisely during the assessment. Don't spend too long on a single question.
- **Online Administration**: Many assessments are conducted online.

Ensure you have a reliable internet connection and a quiet space to focus.
- **Feedback and Scoring**: Some assessments may provide immediate feedback or results, while others might be scored by the employer later. Understand that these scores will be a part of your evaluation process.

Tackling Problem-Solving Exercises

1. What Are Problem-Solving Exercises?

Problem-solving exercises are designed to evaluate your analytical thinking, decision-making, and ability to navigate complex situations. These exercises can take various forms, including case studies, role-playing scenarios, and situational judgment tests.

2. Why Employers Use Problem-Solving Exercises

Employers value problem-solving exercises for several reasons:

- **Real-World Application**: These exercises simulate real workplace scenarios, allowing employers to assess how you approach challenges.
- **Insight into Thought Processes**: Problem-solving exercises reveal how you think, analyze, and arrive at solutions, providing valuable insights into your cognitive processes.
- **Collaboration Skills**: In group settings, these exercises can also showcase your ability to collaborate and communicate effectively with others.

3. Preparing for Problem-Solving Exercises

A. Enhance Your Analytical Skills

- **Practice Analytical Thinking**: Engage in activities that require critical thinking and analysis, such as puzzles, brainteasers, and strategy games.

- **Study Problem-Solving Frameworks**: Familiarize yourself with common problem-solving frameworks, such as SWOT analysis, root cause analysis, and the PDCA (Plan-Do-Check-Act) cycle. Understanding these frameworks can help you structure your approach during exercises.

B. Review Common Case Studies

- **Research Case Studies**: Explore case studies relevant to your industry to understand common challenges and solutions. Analyze how others approached these situations.
- **Mock Exercises**: Participate in mock problem-solving exercises with friends or mentors to practice your skills and receive feedback.

C. Focus on Communication Skills

- **Practice Articulating Your Thought Process**: During problem-solving exercises, it's essential to communicate your reasoning clearly. Practice explaining your thought process aloud.
- **Engage in Group Discussions**: Join discussion groups or forums related to your field. Engaging with others can enhance your ability to collaborate and present your ideas effectively.

4. What to Expect During Problem-Solving Exercises

Problem-solving exercises may vary in format, but here's what you can generally expect:

- **Case Studies**: You may be presented with a business scenario and asked to analyze the problem, propose solutions, and justify your recommendations.
- **Role-Playing**: Some assessments may involve role-playing exercises where you'll interact with an interviewer or other candidates to demonstrate your problem-solving approach.

- **Group Exercises**: In group settings, you may work with other candidates to solve a problem collaboratively. This assesses both your individual contributions and your ability to work as part of a team.

Emotional Intelligence and Personality Tests

1. What Are Emotional Intelligence and Personality Tests?

Emotional intelligence (EI) tests assess your ability to recognize, understand, and manage emotions—both in yourself and others. Personality tests evaluate your character traits, helping employers understand how you might behave in various situations.

2. Why Emotional Intelligence Matters

Emotional intelligence is increasingly recognized as a vital skill in the workplace. Here's why it matters:

- **Team Dynamics**: High emotional intelligence allows you to navigate interpersonal relationships effectively, fostering collaboration and positive team dynamics.
- **Conflict Resolution**: Individuals with strong EI can manage conflicts constructively, leading to better outcomes in challenging situations.
- **Leadership Potential**: Emotional intelligence is often seen as a critical trait for effective leaders. Employers look for candidates who can inspire and motivate others.

3. Preparing for Emotional Intelligence and Personality Tests

A. Understand the Components of Emotional Intelligence

- **Self-Awareness**: Reflect on your emotions and how they impact your behavior. Recognizing your triggers can enhance your emotional

regulation.
- **Self-Management**: Practice techniques for managing stress and emotions. Mindfulness and deep-breathing exercises can be helpful.
- **Social Awareness**: Develop empathy by actively listening to others and seeking to understand their perspectives. Engage in discussions about emotions and feelings.
- **Relationship Management**: Work on building and maintaining positive relationships. Effective communication and conflict resolution skills are essential.

B. Be Authentic in Personality Assessments

- **Answer Honestly**: Approach personality assessments with honesty. Authenticity is key, as employers are looking for a genuine reflection of your personality.
- **Understand the Traits Being Measured**: Familiarize yourself with the personality traits commonly assessed (e.g., openness, conscientiousness, extroversion). Reflect on how these traits relate to your own behavior.

4. What to Expect During Emotional Intelligence and Personality Tests

Emotional intelligence and personality tests can take various forms:

- **Self-Reported Questionnaires**: Many EI and personality assessments are self-reported questionnaires, where you rate your agreement with statements about your behavior and preferences.
- **Situational Judgments**: You may be presented with scenarios and asked to select the most appropriate response based on your emotional understanding.
- **Assessment Feedback**: Some tests provide immediate feedback, while others may be evaluated later by employers. Understanding the feedback can help you prepare for future assessments.

CHAPTER 16: PREPARING FOR BEHAVIORAL ASSESSMENTS

Preparing for behavioral assessments is a critical component of the job search process. By understanding the nature of psychometric tests, honing your problem-solving skills, and developing emotional intelligence, you position yourself as a well-rounded candidate capable of excelling in interviews and assessments.

Approach these assessments with confidence, knowing that preparation and self-awareness are key to your success. As you navigate the assessment process, remember that these tests are not just about evaluating your skills but also about finding a fit for both you and the employer. By leveraging the insights gained from this chapter, you can tackle behavioral assessments with clarity and poise, ultimately enhancing your chances of securing your desired role.

Conclusion: Your Road to Success

As you reach the conclusion of this journey through the multifaceted world of interviewing, it's essential to take a moment to reflect on the comprehensive strategies we've explored. The job market is a dynamic landscape, constantly evolving with new technologies, trends, and expectations. Thus, equipping yourself with the right tools and techniques is not merely advantageous; it's essential for standing out in today's competitive environment. This conclusion serves as a final synthesis of the key strategies discussed throughout the book and offers guidance on how to maintain your growth trajectory as you advance in your career.

Putting It All Together

Recap of Key Strategies

In this book, we've navigated the many facets of preparing for interviews, from crafting an exceptional resume to mastering non-verbal communication and emotional intelligence. Let's recap some of the pivotal strategies that can propel you toward success:

1. **Understanding the Modern Job Market**: Recognizing the shifts in hiring practices due to AI, automation, and online platforms sets the foundation for your approach. Stay informed about what employers seek and how to align your skills and traits accordingly.
2. **Crafting a Stand-Out Resume**: Tailoring your resume to each job

application is critical. Highlight your achievements with measurable results and design your document for readability and impact. Your resume is often your first impression, so make it count.

3. **Perfecting the Cover Letter**: A compelling cover letter can resonate with hiring managers. Avoid common pitfalls and tell your story in a way that showcases your qualifications while making a personal connection to the organization.
4. **Researching the Company and Industry**: Before your interview, invest time in understanding the company culture, industry trends, and networking with current employees. This knowledge will empower you to engage thoughtfully and demonstrate your genuine interest.
5. **Preparing for Common Interview Questions**: Distinguishing between behavioral and situational questions is crucial. Use the STAR method to structure your responses effectively, and practice articulating your answer to the "Tell me about yourself" question in a way that leaves a lasting impression.
6. **Mastering Non-Verbal Communication**: Body language speaks volumes. Your posture, gestures, and eye contact convey confidence, while your appearance can align with the company culture. Learn to read the interviewer's body language as well.
7. **Answering Tough Interview Questions**: Prepare for challenging queries, such as addressing gaps in employment and discussing weaknesses. Frame your answers positively and turn potential negatives into opportunities for growth.
8. **Standing Out in Virtual Interviews**: The shift to virtual interviews demands technical preparation, etiquette awareness, and ways to maintain energy and engagement through the screen. Ensure your setup is flawless and be intentional about your non-verbal cues.
9. **Asking Insightful Questions**: Demonstrating your research through thoughtful questions can set you apart. Probing about the company's challenges positions you as a solution, while inquiries about company culture reveal your interest in a good fit.
10. **Demonstrating Soft Skills**: In a world that increasingly values

interpersonal skills, showcasing emotional intelligence, collaboration, and adaptability is vital. Employers seek team players who can navigate complex social dynamics.

11. **Following Up After the Interview**: Writing a thoughtful thank-you note reinforces your interest and qualifications. Knowing when and how to follow up can keep you in the minds of hiring managers, while handling rejections gracefully can open future doors.
12. **Interviewing for Leadership Roles**: Preparing for leadership positions requires demonstrating strategic thinking and framing your experiences to reflect your vision and decision-making capabilities. Build your personal brand and present yourself as a leader.
13. **Handling Group and Panel Interviews**: Manage multiple interviewers by engaging effectively, balancing attention, and showcasing your collaborative spirit during group exercises.
14. **Overcoming Nerves and Anxiety**: Mental preparation techniques, visualization, and managing imposter syndrome are essential for presenting your best self. Cultivating a positive mindset can significantly impact your performance.
15. **Leveraging Your Network for Success**: Networking is a powerful tool for job seekers. Use your professional connections for referrals and recommendations, maintain relationships after interviews, and gather insider information that could help your application.
16. **Preparing for Behavioral Assessments**: Understanding psychometric tests, honing problem-solving skills, and developing emotional intelligence can prepare you for various assessments that employers may utilize in their selection process.

These strategies collectively form a comprehensive toolkit for navigating the job search process and excelling in interviews. The insights gleaned throughout this book should serve as a foundation upon which you can build your unique approach to job searching and interviewing.

CONCLUSION: YOUR ROAD TO SUCCESS

How to Keep Refining Your Approach

1. **Reflect and Adapt**: Regularly evaluate your interview performance and experiences. After each interview, take note of what went well and what could be improved. This reflection will help you refine your approach for future opportunities.
2. **Seek Feedback**: Don't hesitate to ask for feedback from interviewers or mentors. Constructive criticism can provide valuable insights into your strengths and areas for growth.
3. **Engage in Mock Interviews**: Practicing with friends, family, or career coaches can help you hone your skills. Mock interviews simulate real scenarios, allowing you to receive feedback in a supportive environment.
4. **Stay Updated on Industry Trends**: The job market is always evolving. Subscribe to industry publications, attend webinars, and participate in workshops to keep your skills relevant and your knowledge current.
5. **Continuous Learning**: Invest in your professional development by pursuing certifications, attending courses, or engaging in self-directed learning. Lifelong learning is key to staying competitive in your field.
6. **Network Actively**: Your professional network is a powerful resource. Attend networking events, join industry associations, and leverage social media platforms like LinkedIn to connect with professionals in your field.

Continuing Your Growth

The journey doesn't end once you secure a job; it's merely the beginning of a long and fulfilling career. Continuing your growth involves a commitment to self-improvement and a proactive approach to career development. Here are some essential strategies to ensure you keep moving forward:

1. **Embrace Feedback**: Be open to receiving feedback from colleagues, supervisors, and mentors. Constructive criticism can provide insights that help you identify your strengths and areas for improvement.

2. **Set Goals**: Establish short-term and long-term career goals. These goals can guide your professional development and keep you focused on your growth trajectory. Regularly revisit and adjust your goals as needed.
3. **Stay Informed About Industry Changes**: The world of work is rapidly changing, and staying informed about industry trends is crucial. Follow thought leaders, read relevant literature, and engage with professionals in your field to remain current.
4. **Cultivate a Growth Mindset**: Embrace challenges and view setbacks as opportunities for learning. A growth mindset fosters resilience and adaptability, which are invaluable traits in today's ever-evolving job market.
5. **Expand Your Skill Set**: In addition to soft skills, focus on building technical competencies that are relevant to your field. As industries evolve, new technologies and methodologies emerge, and staying proficient is essential for success.
6. **Network for Opportunities**: Cultivate relationships within your industry. Attend conferences, workshops, and networking events to connect with like-minded professionals. Your network can be a source of new opportunities and insights.
7. **Seek Out Mentorship**: Finding a mentor can significantly impact your professional development. A mentor can provide guidance, share experiences, and offer insights into navigating your career path effectively.
8. **Balance Professional and Personal Growth**: While focusing on career advancement is essential, don't neglect personal development. Engage in activities that enhance your overall well-being, such as pursuing hobbies, volunteering, or spending quality time with loved ones.

The road to success in the job market is not a straight path; it is often winding and filled with challenges. However, by equipping yourself with the strategies outlined in this book and committing to continuous growth, you can navigate this landscape with confidence and resilience. Remember, every interview is an opportunity for learning, every setback can lead to a breakthrough, and every connection you make has the potential to open doors.

As you embark on your journey toward career success, embrace the power of preparation, self-awareness, and adaptability. Stand tall and showcase your unique strengths, and let your passion shine through in every interaction. With dedication and a strategic approach, you are well on your way to achieving your professional aspirations and thriving in the ever-changing world of work.

In conclusion, your road to success is shaped by your actions, your mindset, and your commitment to growth. So, step forward with confidence and make your mark in the professional world. The future is yours to seize!

www.ingramcontent.com/pod-product-compliance
Lightning Source LLC
Chambersburg PA
CBHW071058240526
45471CB00016B/2061